CLARE

Selected Poems and Prose

Oxford University Press, Ely House, London W.1

GLASGOW NEW YORK TORONTO MELBOURNE WELLINGTON
CAPE TOWN IBADAN NAIROBI DAR ES SALAAM LUSAKA ADDIS ABABA
DELHI BOMBAY CALCUTTA MADRAS KARACHI LAHORE DACCA
KUALA LUMPUR SINGAPORE HONG KONG TOKYO

CLARE

SELECTED POEMS AND PROSE

Chosen and edited by

ERIC ROBINSON

and

GEOFFREY SUMMERFIELD

OXFORD UNIVERSITY PRESS

Cover portrait by William Hilton

First published 1966
Reprinted 1970, 1972, 1974

.

Printed photolitho in Great Britain by
J. W. Arrowsmith Ltd., Bristol

To Alexander Bell

ACKNOWLEDGEMENTS

WE WISH to thank the Peterborough Museum Society and the Northampton Public Library Committee for permission to publish from their extensive collections of Clare manuscripts, and we owe a special debt to Dr. Alexander Bell at Peterborough and to Mr. Howard Halliday, Northampton Public Librarian, and his staff, for their enthusiasm and helpfulness over many years.

We wish to thank also Miss Ann Botham for the loan of J. Cary's Map of Northamptonshire, 1789.

Miss Pauline Higgins, History Department Secretary, University of Manchester, has been our tireless and accurate typist.

Finally we wish to thank Professor F. Kermode, Winterstoke Professor of English, University of Bristol, and Professor J. D. Jump for their encouragement of our studies of Clare, which has certainly lightened our burden.

The copyright of Clare's unpublished works is owned by Mr. Eric Robinson.

ERIC ROBINSON
GEOFFREY SUMMERFIELD

CONTENTS

The titles of poems are Clare's except when given
in square brackets.

INTRODUCTION

IN EVERY generation since 1820, when Clare's first book of
poetry was published by John Taylor, the publisher of Keats
and Lamb, and received considerable though condescending
acclaim from the reviewers, there have been some who have
listened attentively to his distinctive voice. But while the
names of Keats and Shelley, Wordsworth, Coleridge, and
Byron, continue to resound in the annals of criticism, Clare
still struggles for a hearing with the general public and even
in the university schools of literary study. The old *Oxford
Book of English Verse* preserved 'I am' (p. 222) from oblivion,
while the school anthologies for very young children kept
alive 'Little Trotty Wagtail' and perhaps one or two other
lyrics from the poet's declining years. But collections of
Clare's prose and verse, affording a truer perspective of his
genius, generally sold slowly and could often be found among
remaindered books. Perceptive critics like Edward Thomas,
Edmund Blunden, J. Middleton Murry, and Geoffrey
Grigson and Robert Graves[1] have made a beginning, in this
century, in the serious criticism of Clare's poetry, but there
is still no single critical work devoted to Clare, and to many
students of poetry he remains unknown. Yet Clare is a great
poet, and no small part of his greatness is, as Robert Graves
has shown, that he held firmly to his poetic vision throughout
a long life, while some like Wordsworth and Southey
faltered, and others like Keats and Shelley died very young.
Inertia is a dreadful natural force. Southey, who is read even
less than Clare, is firmly enshrined by the encyclopaedias and

[1] See Select Bibliography.

literary histories in the Pantheon, while Clare, probably more happy there, is pottering about in the garden outside.

Yet Clare is the most accessible of poets, because he is free of pretension and almost always writes about the things he knows well and which are a part of his life. Apart from a few short visits to London and his brief confinement in the asylum at High Beech in Epping Forest, he spent almost his entire life in his native county of Northamptonshire. Even there, in that one county, his whole experience centred on the years of his childhood and early manhood in the little village of Helpstone. Thus the whole of his spiritual life is in a sense confined to within a day's walking distance in every direction radiating from Helpstone, though there are a few topographical poems about Boston Stump and other places in the neighbouring county of Lincolnshire. Since he came to be known as 'the Northamptonshire Peasant Poet', Clare was doubly damned from the beginning—damned because he was associated with one locality at a time when the railways were breaking down regional boundaries and regional consciousness; and damned because he was a peasant at a time when the national imagination was being captured by the immensity of industrialism. Wordsworth's allegiance to rural Cumberland was first trumpeted a generation before Clare's first volume, and perhaps was easily acceptable because it came from a man of education and could be seen as part of a literary convention. But Clare was not only loyal to the countryside, he was part of it—a whopstraw, another Robert Bloomfield, smelling of the farmyard.

Much of Clare's strength, however, lies in his sense of his roots, his awareness of his own landscape, the directness with which he always sees the places of his childhood. The poem 'Remembrances' (p. 193) brings together many of the places which, elsewhere in Clare's work, earned a poem or poems to themselves. In this poem, however, they are used as a sort of incantation whose power can only be fully appreciated after much browsing in Clare's very extensive poetic output. Langley bush, Eastwell's boiling spring, old Cross Berry way, pleasant Swordy Well, the hollow ash, Sneap Green, Puddocks Nook, Hilly Snow; they are not names alone to Clare, but experiences. Some of these places can still be located on enclosure maps, and even on the modern ordnance maps, but other landmarks, such as trees, have succumbed to time. One tree, however, which can still be pinpointed is 'Salter's Tree' (p. 186) which grew near Castor, but Clare's poetry is full of regrets for other well-known trees that fell to the axe, just as the moorlands were devoured by the plough or the streams were diverted from their natural course in the interests of improved farming. Clare's memory for persons and places was the memory of a saga-teller. There is a letter written from Northampton Asylum in which he asks to be remembered to all the friends of his youth in Helpstone, and the names come flooding from his pen as though he were standing before their cottages and calling them out. Because his vision is always so sharp, whether he writes about a person or a bird's nest, and his memory so reliable, there is a strength in his poetry which seldom allows him to become merely sentimental.

But places have a deeper significance in Clare's poetry than the places that most of us would think of as our map of childhood from which, if we rack our memories, we can remember the name of the street in which we lived, the field where we lit our first illicit bonfire, or the lanes along which we strolled to school. For the map was changed for Helpstone, as well as for many more midland villages, not only by time but also by enclosure. The 'landscape plotted and pieced', about which Hopkins wrote in the later nineteenth century, was largely the product of eighteenth-century and early nineteenth-century enclosure. And so Clare lamented:

> But now alls fled and flats of many a dye
> That seemed to lengthen with the following eye
> Moors loosing from the sight far smooth and blea
> Where swept the plover in its pleasure free
> Are vanished now with commons wild and gay . . .
>
> (*The Mores*, p. 188)

Enclosure changed the landscape, and, in Clare's opinion, destroyed a way of life, not only by tearing up trees and damming brooks, but also by uprooting old customs and changing the social links between master and man. His long satiric poem, *The Parish*, from which we have only space for a few short extracts, is taken up with the evil social effects of enclosure, the inflationary agriculture of the Napoleonic Wars, and the changed status of the local Anglican parson. Even if he were not a fine poet, Clare's observations would be of great value to the historian, since his is almost the only voice that can still be heard from the otherwise silent peasantry of the enclosure years. Even Cobbett, close as his observation is, wrote as a comparative outsider. Clare's remarks help to explain why Anglicanism suffered some of its most severe setbacks in the very rural areas where it might have been expected to be strongest.[1] Similarly, Clare's observations on the old Poor Law institutions of his neighbourhood show them to have possessed much of the severity often said to be the consequence of the Poor Law Reform Act of 1834. As for the customs and the social structure of the early nineteenth-century Northamptonshire village, there is no historical work which could possibly bring them to life as vividly as some of

[1] W. R. Ward, 'The Tithe Question in England in the Early Nineteenth Century', *Journal of Ecclesiastical History*, XVI, 1, 1965.

Clare's poems and prose passages do. (See below; 'Valentine Eve', pp. 100–12, 'The Cellar Door', pp. 89–94, 'A Sunday with Shepherds and Herdboys', and the long passage about the Farmer and the Vicar, pp. 73–81.) Moreover certain sides of peasant life in Clare's period could only be appreciated fully by someone with first-hand knowledge like his. Thus, for example, while it is true that enclosure afforded additional employment in hedging and ditching, Clare, who worked as a member of a gang planting new quick-set hedges, knew from personal experience that it was no job for a married man, because it was itinerant and forced him to sleep abroad, sometimes even in the fields. The hero of his poem, 'Valentine Eve', poses as a wandering Irish harvest worker:

> When the poor irish from their country roves
> And like scotch cattle throng the road in droves

How much social and economic history is concentrated in those two lines, with their reference to migrant Irish farm labour and to the Scottish cattle trade.[1] Clare not only observed his environment but had the wit to know what was significant in it, so that to the discerning eye there is a greater width of reference in his verse and prose than he has ever been given credit for. The famous social historians, the Hammonds, were not at fault in quoting from Clare in their classic *The Village Labourer*, but only in not quoting enough, though it must be remembered that they only knew what had been published of Clare's work in 1911.

If the countryside about Helpstone was not only the map of Clare's boyhood but also part of a rural landscape cruelly altered by enclosure, it was something even more significant.

---

[1] For one of the finest contemporary descriptions of a Scotch drover, see E. Robinson and G. Summerfield (ed.), *John Clare: The Shepherd's Calendar*, (Oxford, 1964), pp. 76–77.

Helpstone was Clare's Paradise, his Garden of Eden. This observation is no literary conceit but plain truth. There is a similarity here between Wordsworth's philosophy in the 'Ode on the Intimations of Immortality' and Clare's imaginative position; but Clare goes much further than Wordsworth in actually identifying the fields of his boyhood with Eden—even, he says, with something more than Eden:

> I sat beside the pasture stream
>   When Beautys self was sitting by
> The fields did more than Eden seem
>   Nor could I tell the reason why

In the landscape of Eden before the Fall, Clare's boyhood love Mary Joyce, is present—she is the Eve to Clare's Adam. Unless we recognize that this is the conscious pattern of imagery in Clare's poetry, we are bound to miss a great deal of his point. Everything in his boyhood environment assumes a new character, a vividness far beyond accurate natural history, a deeper identity because it is part of what Clare calls 'Loves register'. In this 'register', not just trees, but every single tree, not just grass but every single blade of grass is a special act of the Creator and participates in the freshness before the Fall. This is where Middleton Murry, one of the best critics of Clare, goes astray, when, writing of the differences between Clare and Wordsworth, he says that Clare in some ways was a truer poet than Wordsworth, because he had

a truer ear and a more exquisite instinct for words; *but he had nothing of the principle of inward growth which gives to Wordsworth's most careless work a place within the unity of a great scheme.* Wordsworth's incessant effort to comprehend experience would itself have been incomprehensible to Clare.[1]

[1] J. Middleton Murry, *Countries of the Mind*, London, 1937, p. 71. Our italics.

Wordsworth's effort would not have been incomprehensible to Clare because he had made, himself, the same effort. This can best be seen by examining Clare's poetry extensively, but it can be illustrated, to a limited degree, in this selection also. Thus, in 'Shadows of Taste', he writes:

> Some in recordless rapture love to breath[e]
> Natures wild Eden wood and field and heath (p. 152)

and in 'The Morning Wind':

> Theres more then music in this early wind
> Awaking like a bird refreshed from sleep
> And joy what Adam might in eden find
> When he with angels did communion keep (p. 175)

The daisies, he tells us, in 'The Flitting' (p. 201) are as old as Adam and were there when the earth first beheld the sun. Sometimes the allusions to this Eden are explicit, but quite often it is the sharpness of Clare's vision alone that serves to remind us of the 'great scheme' to which his experience belonged.

The recognition of Clare's effort to comprehend his experience in a scheme of imagery would have come more quickly if critics had been more humble towards him. Instead, they have too often stressed Clare's lack of education and his village upbringing, and so have mesmerized themselves into believing that Clare was incapable of sustained thought. But, to put it in the simplest terms, Clare was very well read. His observations of nature often reminded him of his own reading. (See prose passage, p. 56.) He shared in that culture of the great house which descended by devious routes to the cottages, through servants and servants' servants, down to the very poor. It produced not only a society of good manners but also here and there the man and woman of humble station who had read more than the three or four great classics of the cottage shelf—the Bible, *Paradise Lost*, *Pilgrim's Progress*, and *Robinson Crusoe*. Clare's friends among the servants at the Fitzwilliam residence at Milton included Artis and Henderson, who were men of considerable culture, well read in their master's great library, and keenly interested in the antiquities and the natural history of the locality. He was accepted by them as their intellectual equal and they all shared many discoveries together, as well as lending each other books. Clare's library, or the greater part of it, still exists in Northampton Public Library,[1] and there is many an educated man today who possesses a poorer collection of books. Not only was he comparatively *widely* read in the English poetry of the eighteenth century, and in some of the poetry of the seventeenth century, but he was *deeply* read. What he read he made part of himself. His favourite authors, Thomson and Cowper, together with the Bible, may well have provided him with the framework of his ideas about Eden, but he carried those ideas into his own village fields. It may be natural for a shepherd to compare himself to the Jewish pastoralist of the Scriptures, and it was also a fairly common literary comparison in eighteenth-century poetry, but Clare gives life to the commonplace, and writes of sheep-shearing in June with the familiarity that lends authority to his description of social amity at the sheep-shearing feast.[2] In this way, reading and experience go hand in hand, as they do in Shakespeare's *The Winter's Tale*.

While enclosure brought a sense of alienation to village life, Clare's own stability, mental and physical, was threatened by a number of personal factors, of which the two most important were the separation from Mary Joyce, and later,

[1] D. Powell, *Catalogue of the John Clare Collection in the Northampton Public Library*, Northampton, 1964, pp. 23–34.

[2] See his *Shepherd's Calendar*, pp. 65–67.

the move from Helpstone to Northborough. We cannot be certain why Clare and Mary parted, but it looks as if her father felt that Clare was her social inferior and that the relationship ought to be broken. Clare does not seem to have held Mary herself quite blameless in the matter, though his attitude varies in different poems. However that may be, Mary remained for the rest of his days the symbol of innocence, the Eve of his Eden, the First Love which was to be the touchstone for all later experience. That is why we have made 'Dedication to Mary', hitherto unpublished, the first poem of this book. When he went mad, Clare believed that he was married to Mary, as well as to his real wife, Patty, and that he was imprisoned because of his bigamy. His love for Mary did not cause him to hate Patty (whose proper name was Martha Turner), but he regarded the two women as the Mary and Martha, in a scriptural sense, of his life. He wrote many poems to Mary, long after they had parted, and even long after she was dead, but did we not know this from other evidence, the poems would give us no hint of this fantastic situation. We might conclude from them that Clare was in fact married to Mary and was writing the poems to his living wife. But this is only of biographical interest: what is more important from the literary point of view, is that Mary always elicits the very best from Clare's pen. The intense vision of some of Clare's asylum poems derives from Mary (see below, p. 220), and even when he writes, as he often does, of other girls, one can see that it is really Mary who inspires him. No other poet has ever managed to preserve inviolate the image of first love as Clare contrived to do, and for this reason alone he deserves a special place in the affections of the young. The earlier poems to Mary show the poet struggling to reconcile himself to the separation from her and to his deep sense of loss, but when all his other troubles of poverty, uprooting, and lack of public recognition fell upon him, his mind was unable to keep separate at all times the world of reality and the world of his soul's longing, in which Mary still lived and still was his.

Mary and Helpstone, Nature before enclosure, Eve before the Temptation, Eden before the Fall, childhood before the onset of adult trials and deceptions, were therefore a unity in Clare's mind. Clare lived to experience a constant struggle between his vision of unity and all the discordant realities which broke it down, and which seemed in consequence to threaten the meaning of his existence. His first success came to him when his first volume of poetry was published in 1820, but that success was soured by the fact that Mary was no longer there to share it with him. Consoling himself with Martha Turner, he made her pregnant, and his sense of responsibility led him to marry her. She remained illiterate to the end of her days, always signing her name with a mark, and there are several indications that Clare did not always consider his wife and himself to be well suited to each other. Nevertheless she bore him several children and faced many years of hardship with him and without him. But the marriage did not begin auspiciously, and Clare had at least one other affair after his marriage. In addition, Clare's relationships with his patrons and his publishers were far from happy. Lord Radstock, an active, proselytizing Evangelical, helped Clare with great energy, but also bombarded him with comments on how he should conduct his spiritual life, his obligations to the opulent classes, and the ingratitude of his criticizing those in authority. 'I must confess that I discover in his character a want of gratitude and proper feeling towards the opulent and higher orders which has lower'd him not a little in my opinion': Radstock to Taylor, 30 March 1820. Clare resented his interference but was too much at a social

disadvantage to remonstrate with his patron. He was reluct-
antly obliged to defer in several matters to him and to
Radstock's friend, Mrs. Emmerson, whose rather silly
emendations are littered over quite a number of Clare's
manuscripts. In particular, Radstock and Mrs. Emmerson
strongly objected to the vulgarity of Clare's muse—a vulgarity
which in fact reflects a certain healthy robustness. John Taylor,
the publisher, felt entitled to correct Clare's grammar, his
rhyme-schemes, and his vocabulary, so that they would
accord with the polite taste of the period. He was probably
doing the only thing possible at the time, since this was a
period, after 1820, when standards of correctness in spelling
and grammar were becoming more stringent, but the conse-
quences were severe, as we can better appreciate today. In
the early volumes of Clare's poetry, Taylor was persuaded to
allow many of Clare's dialect words to stand where they did
not offend propriety, but by the time of *The Shepherd's
Calendar* in 1827, the publisher was slashing more vigorously,
until almost all Clare's 'provincialisms' were replaced by
words acceptable to London literary taste.[1] Clare, however,
was very much a son of his own village, as we have seen, and
it was therefore natural for him to use the vocabulary of
his everyday speech, especially when it was so much more
telling than the poeticisms of his day. He strongly resented
Taylor's treatment of the language of *The Shepherd's Calendar*,[2]
and it is ironic that two present-day editors of Clare should
write approvingly of Taylor's truncated version:

There are very few dialect words in the *Shepherd's Calendar*, and we
find this deliberate part of his art almost perfected . . .[3]

[1] See E. Robinson and G. Summerfield, 'John Taylor's Editing of Clare's
The Shepherd's Calendar', *Review of English Studies*, New Series, XIV 56,
November 1963, pp. 359–69.
[2] See R. E. S. article cited above.
[3] J. W. and Anne Tibble, *Life of John Clare*, London, 1932, p. 293.

The problem arises as to the way in which Clare should be published today. In this volume we have neither corrected Clare's spelling, grammar, nor punctuation, but have contented ourselves with referring the reader to the glossary wherever we thought that there might be obscurity. Once the business of correction is begun there is no end, and the editor soon finds himself trying to rewrite Clare's verse for him, in order to make a rhyme-scheme fit in with some modified piece of grammar. Clare makes his views about grammar perfectly clear in a fragment from what appears to be an unpublished essay:

Those who have made grammer up into a system and cut it into classes and orders as the student does the animal or vegetable creation may be a fine recreation for schools but it becomes of no use towards making any one so far acquainted with it as to find it useful—it will only serve to puzzle and mislead to awe and intimidate instead of aiding and encouraging him therefore it pays nothing for the study

A person may be very clever at cutting trees and animals on paper but he is nothing as an artist and a person may be very clever at detecting faults in composition and yet in the writing of it may be a mere cypher him self and one that can do nothing

And such a one as Cobbet who has come boldly forward and not only assailed the outworks of such a pedantic garison but like a skilful general laid open its weakness to all deserves from praise for the use of his labour [more] then all the rest of the castle building grammarians put together for he plainly comes to this conclusion— that what ever is intellig[i]ble to others is grammer and what ever is commonsense is not far from correctness.

The verse is nearly always quite easy to understand. The prose is a little more difficult, because Clare omits full-stops and capital letters, so we have tried the experiment of leaving a gap between sentences. But Clare feels that the most important thing is what a writer has to say, and that if he sets out to say it clearly, the punctuation will look after itself:

> do I write intelligable   I am genneraly understood tho I do not use that awkward squad of pointings called commas colons semicolons etc and for the very reason that altho they are drilled hourly daily and weekly by every boarding school Miss who pretends to gossip in correspondence they do not know their proper exercise for they even set gramarians at loggerheads and no one can assign them the proper places for give each a sentence to point and both shall differ— point it differently

What could be plainer than that? And see how cunningly the comparison with an awkward squad at drill is sustained through the passage. Clare's 'Journey out of Essex' (see below pp. 207–16) is an exemplary piece of direct writing, composed by a man worn out by physical and mental exertion, and the other prose passages in this book are intended to exemplify Clare's qualities as a prose writer. His sense of character and his ability to describe human relationships are shown in the passage about the Farmer and the Vicar (p. 73), his vigour of expression can perhaps be best appreciated in the Cobbett-like 'Apology for the Poor' (p. 190), while every passage of nature description exemplifies his accuracy and directness of evocation. Clare always objected strongly to artificiality of language in poetry and in prose. He objected, for example, to Shenstone's poems on the grounds that 'Putting the Correct Language of the Gentleman into the mouth of a Simple Shepherd or Vulgar Ploughman is far from Natural'.[1] His own writings are free from this vice, and are as innocent of pretension as they are of punctuation. His qualities are well displayed in his letters, where simplicity of style gives warmth and life to everything he writes, and when he chose to follow

[1] J. W. and Anne Tibble (edd.), *Letters of John Clare*, London, 1951, p. 25.

Gilbert White in adopting the letter as his vehicle for writing about natural history, he made a very wise choice.

To the separation from Mary, and to the difficulties which Clare increasingly experienced with his patrons and his publisher, must be added the change in taste of the English reading public in the eighteen-thirties. Taylor saw that there was a falling-off in the demand for poetry and wrote to Clare on 3 August 1827:

The Season has been a very bad one for new Books, and I am afraid the Time has passed away in which Poetry will answer...the Shepherds Calendar has had comparatively no Sale...I think in future I shall confine my Speculations [i.e. financial] to works of Utility...[1]

Taylor began to specialize in textbooks of different kinds, and by 1830 had become bookseller and publisher to the University of London. The poet, Darley, wrote works on mathematics for him, and Taylor's list soon included numerous works on natural science and engineering, the intellectual tools of the Industrial Revolution. It is also probably true that the reading public wanted its literature to be increasingly *about* something, as a friend, to whom we are much indebted, illuminatingly comments in a letter to one of us:

...the new town classes wanted books to be 'about'...and what was Clare 'about'? Nothing exciting like Walter Scott's nuns being walled up and Scotsmen dying at Flodden. Nothing exciting like Byron's Greeks. Nothing exciting like Keats' Italians...We were entering the world of the reviewers, who might have passed Clare if his dialect had reminded them of their Scottish home...He was not for girls—and they, the readers of poetry—who saw soon they preferred the novel—high life seen from below stairs...[2]

[1] Taylor to Clare, 20 November 1827.
[2] E. Welbourne to E. Robinson, 25 June 1965.

New town habits were the death of Clare and his poetry as they were of Clare's world in general. It was a cruel twist of Fate that granted fame to an obscure agricultural labourer and then snatched it out of his grasp, as society, in its tormented sleep, turned its back on him. Taylor was blamed by Clare not only, rightly, for his lack of attention to Clare's concerns, but also, wrongly, for what was out of Taylor's control, a change of taste on the part of the reading public. Something of the change can be seen in the vogue for annuals, —'Keepsakes', 'Forget-Me-Nots', 'Friendship's Offerings' etc.,—which were shipped off to absent relatives in India or to maiden aunts in Lyme Regis, and to which Clare also submitted poems in the hope of earning an occasional half guinea. But man cannot live by candy-floss alone. Clare's family went short, he fell into debt, half-starved himself, and became ill, and, as he thought, friendless. He could no longer return to village society, the shortcomings of which had always been clear to him

> Goosey goosey gander
> Where would you wander
> Up the fen and down the fen
> To cackle and to slander

and just as certainly he was no part of the London literary society of Taylor, Lamb, Reynolds and the other contributors to the *London Magazine*.

At the depths of his misfortunes in 1832, the Fitzwilliam family offered him a cottage, four miles away from Helpstone at Northborough, and Clare was glad to accept it, because it seemed to promise him security. Clare was grateful to the Fitzwilliams for their kindness, and would not have welcomed the criticisms made of them by later writers. He himself was still part of a society in which the great house was the focus.

What Clare failed to realize, however, was the wrench which it would mean to him to move from the cottage where he had spent all his life, the hearth of his native Eden. The move to Northborough is the subject of two of Clare's greatest poems, 'Decay' (pp. 205–07) and 'The Flitting' (pp. 196–204). The first of these poems opens with words which link the two poems together:

> O poesy is on the wane
> For fairey visions all unfitting
> I hardly know her face again
> Nature herself seems on the flitting

Clare is afraid that the springs of his creativeness will have dried up as a consequence of this removal:

> But poesy is passed away
> A withered stalk a naked tree

We have printed 'Decay' and its companion poem, 'The Flitting', in full, so that the reader may appreciate the deracination which Clare felt. Once again, Clare makes it clear in 'The Flitting' that he is speaking of no idealized abstract landscape but of a particular place, by naming Royce Wood, one of his favourite haunts, and the home of his beloved nightingales. Now that he has moved to Northborough it seems to him that:

> The sun een seems to lose its way
> Nor knows the quarter it is in

As he says in 'Decay', when referring to his early days in Helpstone

> I thought the flowers upon the hills
> Were flowers from Adam's open gardens,

whereas, after the flitting:

> The stream it is a common stream
>   Where we on Sundays used to ramble
> The sky hangs oer a broken dream—
>   The bramble's dwindled to a bramble.

It has sometimes been said that Clare shows no development in his work. These two poems are clear proof of the contrary. If we look at the poems from the 1820 volume (pp. 50–63)—and we must emphasize that we have chosen only the best—they lack the much deeper and more reflective note struck in these great poems of 1832. The latter are poems of Clare's maturity, and though they are full of passion and disillusionment, the passion and disillusionment are contained by the firm thought-structure and accomplished verse of a practised poet. The language is less traditionally poetic than that of such a poem as 'Summer Images' (p. 166), which includes among its splendours the language of Gray and Collins—a language later discarded by Clare for words which came more naturally to him. At the same time, in the poetry of this decade, Clare is still in possession of his faculties, and he has not descended to the restricted range of language and subject-matter of his later asylum lyrics, which have perhaps been overvalued as a whole because of the intensity of one or two.

As a poet, Clare was out of his time. He belongs to the world before the French Revolution, and it must be remembered that times changed more slowly in Helpstone than in London where literary fashion was dictated. Clare could admire Pope when it was the done thing among London literary critics to decry him, or Erasmus Darwin, when Canning and his smart friends had made him ridiculous. The judiciousness of Clare's verdicts on literature is an eighteenth-century judiciousness, founded in good sense and balanced emotion. Although Clare read Keats and Wordsworth and Coleridge, it is not these writers to whom he constantly refers, and it is not the Romantics, apart from Byron, the most eighteenth-century in feeling, who provided him with his early models. This can be illustrated by some of his differences with his publisher. Taylor gave the following advice to Clare:

I have often remarked that your Poetry is much the best when you are not describing common things, and if you would raise your Views generally, & speak of the Appearances of Nature each Month more philosophically (if I may so say) or with more Excitement, you would greatly improve these little poems; some parts of November are extremely good—others are too prosaic—they have too much of the language of common everyday Description;—faithful I grant they are, but that is not all—'What in me is low, Raise & refine' is the way in which you should conceive them as addressing you . . .[1]

When he was in a more impatient mood, he spoke of Clare's first version of 'July' of *The Shepherd's Calendar* as 'a descriptive catalogue in rhyming Prose'. Mrs. Emmerson also joined in with talk to Taylor of Clare proving 'himself capable of higher subjects than talking of Birds & flowers'.[2] There was a difference of a generation in taste between Taylor and Mrs. Emmerson on one hand and Clare on the other, as well as a difference in quality of judgement. Quite apart from the fact that Clare had no need to inject philosophy and excitement into his poetry, since the excitement was already there for anyone with half an eye, and the only philosophy required was the consistent framework of thought and feeling in which the whole of Clare's work was already shaped, there still remained a gap between London and Helpstone in the 1820s.

[1] Taylor to Clare, 4 March 1826.
[2] Mrs. Emmerson to Clare, 8 December 1826.

Clare's reading had not led him to despise descriptive
poetry. The Augustans had a place for it and Clare had a taste
for it. Its pace was slower, its conventions were more elaborate
than those of the intense Romantic lyric but its origins were
perfectly respectable. Cowper, whom Clare admired perhaps
above any other poet, had made the descriptive poem a
vehicle not only for his observations of nature but for his
emotional reactions to it. Clare's emotional reactions to
nature are there too, but they are not, except in some very
early poems, the reactions of a leisured gentleman but of a
working man, and when Taylor occasionally managed to
see what Clare's reactions were—to rustic courtship, to
magisterial injustice, to middle-class prudery—he preferred
to strike them out. Later editors of Clare have shared the
post-Romantic enthusiasm for poems of feeling, and so have
tended to discard or to curtail those poems by Clare which do
not accord with their picture of him as a Romantic poet.
Poems in which he is quietly, even ruminatingly, descriptive,
or where he turns to social satire, are set aside as not reflecting
his true genius. Yet *The Shepherd's Calendar* is a magnificent
example of a sustained descriptive poem in the eighteenth-
century tradition. It is based on a month-by-month account
of village and farming life, in which human and natural
events are very carefully interwoven. The human figures in
the landscape are always of importance, and this interest was
intended to be strengthened by following each month's
descriptive poem by a verse tale related to that month. That
is why we have selected from *The Shepherd's Calendar* the
poem for February and 'Valentine Eve' which was the verse-
tale originally intended to accompany it.

The Parish, which has never been published in full, is a
piece of incisive and sustained satire, and by no means dis-
graces Clare, for its portraits are energetic and its criticisms

telling. The informal 'parish council' is neatly pinned to the
wall:

> With learning just enough to sign a name
> And skill sufficient parish rates to frame
> And cunning deep enough the poor to cheat
> This learned body for debatings meet
> Tho many heads the parliment prepare
> And each one claims some wisdom for its share
> Like midnight with her vapours tis so small
> They make but darkness visible withall;

the braggart farmer's son, the fashionable daughter, the
hunting curate, the parish clerk make up a set of characters
which no satirist need be ashamed of. We can see other village
characters in the ballad, 'The Cellar Door' (p. 89) for the
alehouse was always one of Clare's favourite places of resort
and John Barleycorn one of his best friends. He was not a tea-
drinker. If one looks at Hilton's portrait of John Clare as a
young man, one can see in an instant what the nineteenth-
century Romantics—and for that matter, their descendants
in the twentieth century—would like Clare to have been.
The portrait is one of those genetic portraits of Keats, Shelley,
Byron, Rupert Brooke, or who-you-will, that might be
interchanged without anyone being much concerned about
the differences. The poet is handsome by right, curly-haired
and rather fey, but beautifully wholesome in the carefully
arranged disorder of his clothes. The same prettification was
carried out by Hilton on Clare's cottage, so that the poet was
obliged to remark that Hilton 'has forced poor J. C. from his
flail & spade to strut on canvas in the town of humour ... I
will take him from his "water nymphs" to lye on the hobs
of our dirty cottages to be read by every greasy thumbed
wench & chubby clown'.[1]

[1] Clare to Taylor, 20 May 1820.

Clare was never what his critics would like him to have been. He was at one and the same time coarser and more delicate of sentiment than they thought, fonder of his beer and a pretty ankle than they wanted to admit, yet more deeply honourable and responsible than they could imagine, more accurate in his observation than they could judge and more reflective than they could perceive. As a poet he was certainly much more varied in his forms of expression than the usual anthology selected from his poems would suggest.

None of his talents saved him during his lifetime from almost total oblivion. *The Shepherd's Calendar* sold very badly, and Clare was obliged to attempt the publication of *The Midsummer Cushion* by obtaining subscriptions. Although he was still hopeful of success, his increasing ill health forced him to abandon the project, and finally *The Rural Muse* was published in 1835 by How and Whittaker. The beautifully transcribed manuscript of *The Midsummer Cushion* is still preserved by Peterborough Museum Society, and is a monument to Clare's frustrations and failure. We have included in this selection several poems from it (pp. 81–207, *passim*). It is particularly rich in sonnets, a verse-form with which Clare had great success. The sonnets are the pen-and-ink sketches of the great painter—they capture the scene just as the artist saw it before he had time to reflect deeply upon it. Just as the artist's sketches sometimes form the basis of a more finished canvas so Clare's sonnets were sometimes worked upon to make longer poems, but mostly they exist solely for themselves, and their appeal lies in their freshness. They portray birds and their nests, animals, seasons, times of day, and rural labours and recreations. They lie so rich and profuse among his work that it is very difficult to choose from them, and like a child sorting sea-shells in a bucket, one finds it almost impossible to throw one away. It is possible that they also represent for Clare a kind of self-discipline, forcing him to concentrate and obtain his effects with economy, where in other poems he allowed himself to wander a little aimlessly and in a more expansive mood. The measure of his success can be judged by the way in which he arrests the reader's attention with his first lines:

> 'Winter is come in earnest . . .'
> 'I love at eventide to walk alone'
> 'The autumn morning waked by many a gun'
> 'Hugh Elm thy rifted trunk all notched and scarred'
> 'I had a joy and keep it still alive'.

The discipline, however, is sometimes relaxed by his habit of writing two or three sonnets in a sequence as in 'The Flood (p. 164), 'Signs of Winter' (p. 163), and 'The Badger' (p. 126). One would not expect, and generally does not find, any great weight of thought in the sonnets, but they are a series of images, and Clare's images are very evocative. The two sonnets 'Early Images' (p. 174) illustrate this very clearly, where the images of early morning are threaded together like beads on a string. Many of these sonnets found their way into newspapers, and though Clare was seldom paid for their publication, they reached a public which might otherwise have never seen them at all.

The failure to publish *The Midsummer Cushion* and the poor response by the public to *The Rural Muse*, which partly replaced it, meant the end of the road for Clare's ambitions. He had been badly disturbed, now and again, by the 'blue devils' for several years before he entered Matthew Allen's private asylum in Epping Forest, as a voluntary patient, in 1837. He was well treated at High Beech, allowed a considerable amount of freedom, and encouraged to write poetry, but in his disturbed frame of mind he was quite unable to understand why he was separated from Helpstone and his family. He suffered delusions, believing himself at different times to be Ben Caunt, a well-known prizefighter, Lord Byron, Robert Burns, and various other people. To his delusion that he was Byron, whose rebellious personality had always fascinated Clare and whose funeral he had witnessed in London, we owe two poems 'Child Harold' and 'Don Juan' [1] which were begun at High Beech. The first of these poems is a very interesting performance. It is a long poem of nine-line stanzas, interspersed with lyrical poems which explore or intensify the emotions established in the narrative stanzas. It has some of the characteristics of Byron's verse, but it is an attempt by Clare, even in his madness, to get to grips with reality, to ascertain his own personality, and to resolve the conflict between vision and reality. One of his dilemmas in it is to make up his mind about Mary. 'How is it possible', he seems to be asking, 'that Mary, the archetype of innocence and freshness, should abandon me?' Mary's failure to stand by him appears to reflect the hypocrisy and double-dealing of the whole of society, and Clare imagines that it is his own truthfulness which has caused society to turn upon him and to imprison him. The poem moves from intensely detailed personal circumstances to moments of generalization, and at its best attains a glowing quality not unlike that of a Samuel Palmer painting:

> The Paigles Bloom In Showers In Grassy Close
> How Sweet To Be Among Their Blossoms Led
> And Hear Sweet Nature To Herself Discourse
> While Pale The Moon Is Bering Over Head
> And Hear The Grazeing Cattle Softly Tread

[1] For the full text of these poems, see *Later Poems of John Clare,* ed. E. Robinson and G. Summerfield, Manchester, 1964.

Cropping The Hedgerows Newly Leafing Thorn
Sounds Soft As Visions Murmured Oer In Bed
At Dusky Eve or Sober Silent Morn
For Such Delights Twere Happy Man Was Born

The capitalization of the letters is a symptom of Clare's
madness, but the verse itself is entirely lucid in such moments
as these, and indeed there is a kind of sense even in the most
troubled sections of the poem. 'Child Harold' is a haunting
poem and shows Clare still struggling, even in a madhouse,
to make sense of his tragic existence.

Clare ran away from High Beech in 1841 and walked the
whole way back to Northamptonshire to rejoin Mary, who,
he thought, was waiting for him and to whom he had been
writing while he was in the asylum. A few miles from his
home he was collected in a waggon by Patty and taken back
to their cottage. On his return he wrote an account of his
escape, the 'Journey out of Essex' (pp. 207–16), which tells
of his adventures and the hardships he endured. Though he
had come home to Northamptonshire, it was all to no avail,
and a few months later he was certified insane by Dr. Fenwick
Skrimshire and sent to the Northampton General Asylum,
where he spent his days until his death in May 1864. We
might expect the date of this second committal to an asylum,
especially when it was to last the rest of his life, to be the end
of Clare as a poet. Even here, however, Clare defies prediction.
Hundreds of his poems survive from his years at Northampton,
and many more may have been lost. Clare's life at Northampton contrasts with the frightening account of madness in
Jane Eyre. The building where Clare was kept is still standing
and is now a private mental hospital. It is a gracious building
with lofty rooms, and elegant doors and plastered ceilings,
with most beautiful private grounds at the rear of the building.
Clare was allowed a good deal of freedom, often walked into

the town and was a familiar figure to the townspeople sitting in the porch of All Saints' Church. The House Steward of the Asylum, W. F. Knight, was a sensitive man, interested in literature, who gave his friendship to Clare and encouraged him to write, and it is through his interest that so many of Clare's poems written at this time survive, for Knight himself transcribed many of them into two large volumes which are now in Northampton Public Library. Some of the poems are addressed to girls whom Clare met in Northampton, in shops or in ale-houses, as he strolled about the town. Their freshness and youth evoked for him the joys of his early life and of his association with Mary, and it is fitting that these otherwise obscure young friends of his should gain an immortality in his poetry.

Though most of the poems written in his closing years are love songs or ballads, and though most of them, at least superficially, speak of enjoyments in nature, felt in the past or even in the present, a sombre note is occasionally struck. The consequence of free will in Adam's Paradise was the Fall and the introduction of sin into the world. Thus the time would come when there would be a terrible Day of Judgement. The sequence is followed in 'Spring' in Thomson's *Seasons*: first a picture of Eden, showing the contentment of rural society, enjoying cheerful labour and refreshed by song; then the Fall where all the harmony of Eden is destroyed; and then the Deluge and the Day of Judgement. In Clare's poetry, the theme of Judgement, which had always been there, grew stronger and gained fuller expression in his later years. In 1841 he wrote the apocalyptic poem:

> There is a day a dreadful day
> Still following the past
> When sun and moon are past away
> And mingle with the blast

> There is a vision in my eye
> A vacuum oer my mind
> Sometimes as on the sea I lye
> Mid roaring waves and wind

Imitations of the psalms often follow a similar trend, and
thunder and shipwreck are frequent subjects. His early
reading of Falconer's *Shipwreck* and similar works now
provided him with an imagery of terror. 'An invite to Eternity' (p. 223) asks the maiden to go with the poet:

> Where the path hath lost its way
> Where the sun forgets the day

and

> Where stones will turn to flooding streams
> Where plains will rise like ocean waves
> Where life will fade like visioned dreams
> And mountains darken into caves

Even the poems which ostensibly deal with lighter matters
like the poem about the lady-bird or 'Clock a Clay' (p. 227)
may have a disturbing note of fear and insecurity about them,
while the famous 'I am' (p. 222) speaks of 'the living sea of
waking dreams'. There is no question that Clare in his later
years developed a very distinctive voice, an unmistakeable
intensity and vibrance, such as the later pictures by Van Gogh
possess, but we must also guard against attributing too much
importance to the poems of his madness because we live in an
age fascinated by the problems of mental stress. It is salutary,
after reading some of the last poems, to turn back to a poem
like 'Sabbath Bells' (p. 180) where the free response of Clare
to Nature is untinged by despair and doubt, or to the Augustan
calm of 'Summer Images' (p. 166) or 'The Nightingales Nest'
(p. 119). And when one does so, it is the continuity of Clare's

life and ways of thought and feeling which claims one's attention, rather than the disruptions of insanity.

Finally it ought to be remembered that Clare would still have been one of the finest poets of his century if he had died in 1837 before he had entered an asylum. His published work at that time was already a considerable achievement, even though it had been tampered with by Taylor. And even in 1837 there were many poems still in manuscript which had never been published and none of Clare's prose had been published at all. He was a most prolific and fertile writer, and could perhaps be called 'the green man of English poetry'. His work is still read a hundred years after his death and his fame will grow when his work is presented in a form which will make some overall estimate of it possible. Clare asked for no pretentious gravestone. He felt that if his work lived, then an imposing tombstone would be unnecessary; if his work did not live, then no tombstone, however elaborate, would save him from oblivion. There is no doubt that Clare will live.

CLARE'S LIFE

1792 Shelley born.
1793 John Clare born at Helpstone, Northants, 13 July.
1794 Blake's *Songs of Experience*. Erasmus Darwin's *Zoönomia*.
1795 Keats born. Speenhamland.
1796 Death of Burns.
1797 Bewick's *History of British Birds*.
1798 Battle of the Nile. *Lyrical Ballads*. Cowper: *On the Receipt of my Mother's Picture*.
1799 Religious Tract Society founded.
1800 Bloomfield's *The Farmer's Boy*. Death of Cowper.
1802 Scott's *Minstrelsy of the Scottish Border*. Bloomfield's *Rural Tales*.
1803 Hayley's *Life of Cowper*.
1804 Napoleon proclaimed Emperor.
1805 Cary's translation of Dante's *Inferno*. Battle of Trafalgar (21 October).
1806 Roscoe's *The Butterfly's Ball and Grasshopper's Feast*; Byron's *Fugitive Pieces*.
1807 Kirke White's *Remains*.
1808 Byron sails for the Mediterranean.
1809 Battle of Corunna; Enclosure Act for Helpstone.
1810 Crabbe's *The Borough*.
1811 Luddite Riots. Bloomfield's *The Banks of the Wye*.
1812 Byron's *Childe Harold* (I and II).
1813 Coleridge's *Remorse*.
1814 Cary completes his translation of Dante's *Divina Commedia*.

1815 Waterloo: Napoleon exiled to St. Helena. Byron's *Hebrew Melodies*.

1816 Shelley's *Alastor*.

1817 Keats's *Poems*.

1818 Keats's *Endymion*.

1820 Publication of *Poems Descriptive of Rural Life and Scenery*. Marriage to Martha Turner.

1821 *Poems Descriptive*, Fourth Edition. *The Village Minstrel and other Poems*. Taylor acquires the *London Magazine*. Death of Keats.

1822 Death of Shelley.

1823 Death of Octavius Gilchrist. Elizabeth Kent's *Flora Domestica*.

1824 Death of Byron. First number of Alaric Watt's *Literary Souvenir*. Taylor withdraws from the *London Magazine*.

1825 Cunningham's *Songs of Scotland, Ancient and Modern*. Death of Lord Radstock. Taylor and Hessey dissolve their partnership.

1826 Hone's *Every Day Book*.

1827 Publication of *The Shepherd's Calendar, with Village Stories and Other Poems*.

1828 Lockhart's *Life of Burns*.

1829 Hogg's *The Shepherd's Calendar*; Tennyson's *Timbuctoo*.

1830 Publication of Dr. Matthew Allen's *Cases of Insanity*. Moore's *Life of Byron*. Captain Swing Riots.

1831 Ebenezer Elliott's *Corn-Law Rhymes*.

1832 Clare leaves Helpstone and moves to Northborough. Reform Act.

1834 Poor Law Reform Act.

1835 Publication of *The Rural Muse*.

1837 Publication of Dr. Matthew Allen's *Classification of the*

Insane; Clare removed to High Beech, Epping. Accession of Queen Victoria.

1841   Clare escapes from High Beech (July) and is removed to Northampton (December).

1845   W. F. Knight appointed House Steward, Northampton Asylum.

1849   Death of Thomas Inskip, and of Peter De Wint.

1850   W. F. Knight leaves Northampton for Birmingham.

1864   Clare dies at Northampton, May 20th. John Taylor dies.

1865   W. B. Yeats born.

SELECT BIBLIOGRAPHY

The recent editions of the poetry:

Geoffrey Grigson (ed.): *Poems of John Clare's Madness* (London, 1949).
Textually a very unreliable volume; but it contains a most
illuminating Introduction.

Geoffrey Grigson (ed.): *Selected Poems* (Muses' Library, 1950).
Approximately a third of the text draws on the unreliable
readings of *Poems of John Clare's Madness.*

J. W. Tibble (ed.): *The Poems of John Clare* (London, 1935).
A fairly comprehensive *selection* of Clare's poetry; textually, an
amalgam of earlier, improved, editions and manuscript sources;
inadequately annotated and very far from a definitive edition.

J. W. and A. Tibble (edd.): *Selected Poems* (Everyman, 1965).
An unsatisfactory volume which reprints Taylor's truncated
text of *The Shepherd's Calendar* and which is editorially incon-
sistent in its handling of the text of the later poems.

Eric Robinson and Geoffrey Summerfield (edd.): *The Later Poems*
(Manchester, 1964).
An attempt to present Clare's work of the asylum years in the
form in which he wrote it.

Eric Robinson and Geoffrey Summerfield (edd.): *The Shepherd's
Calendar* (Oxford, 1964).
A reclamation of Clare's most ambitious single poem from the
available MS. sources.

Biographical:

Frederick W. Martin: *The Life of John Clare*, 2nd edn., with an
Introduction and Notes by Eric Robinson and Geoffrey
Summerfield (London, 1964).
This remains the freshest and most illuminating of the bio-
graphies.

43

J. L. Cherry: *Life and Remains of John Clare* (London and Northampton, 1873).

An indifferent biography, but the volume is interesting for its 220 pages of Clare's later poetry and prose, even though the text is bowdlerized.

Edmund Blunden (ed.): *Sketches in the Life of John Clare* (London, 1931).

A well edited selection from the mass of Clare's autobiographical notes.

Edmund Blunden: *Keats's Publisher, A Memoir of John Taylor* (London, 1936).

An interesting and lucid account of Clare's publisher, but rather over-generous in its appraisal of Taylor's treatment of his authors.

J. W. and A. Tibble: *John Clare, A Life* (London, 1932).

A comprehensive, detailed biography, now superseded in matters of detail by the same authors' *John Clare: His Life and Poetry* (London, 1956).

Critical and Textual:

Edward Thomas: *Feminine Influence on the Poets* (London, n.d.)

John Middleton Murry: *John Clare and Other Studies* (London, 1950).

John Middleton Murry: *Unprofessional Essays* (London, 1956).

Kenneth Richmond: *Poetry and the People* (London, 1947).

C. Day Lewis: *The Lyric Impulse* (London, 1965).

Robert Graves: *The Crowning Privilege* (Penguin, 1959).

Anne Elizabeth Baker: *Glossary of Northamptonshire Words and Phrases* (London and Northampton, 1854, 2 vols.).

A comprehensive and detailed attempt to cope with the riches of Clare's dialect, based in part on a reading of Clare's poetry and on interviews with him in the Asylum at Northampton.

NOTE ON THE TEXT

THE text is everywhere taken from the original manuscripts but the full editorial apparatus is reserved for our projected edition of Clare's poetry in the Oxford English Text Series. For the few early poems, first published in 1820, the existing manuscripts are heavily corrected for spelling and punctuation, sometimes by Clare, presumably on someone else's advice, or by another hand, and do not seem to be the manuscripts from which the published text was prepared. Accordingly in these poems we have supplemented the manuscripts by printing lines from the first edition and enclosing them in square brackets [   ].

Where a dialect word or a confusing misspelling occurs we have referred the reader to the Glossary by an asterisk * but this is only done when the word occurs for the first time in this volume, in order to avoid littering the text. When in doubt the reader is advised to consult the Glossary. We also give a special warning about Clare's habit of omitting the apostrophe in such phrases as: I'm, we'll, they'll etc.

Prose passages have been left unpunctuated, but, to assist the reader, a gap is left between sentences. In the list of contents it will be observed that the titles of prose passages have been indented.

Clare's country in the late eighteenth century.

Dedication to ★ ★ ★ ★

O M ★ ★ ★ thou that once made all
What youthful dreams coud pleasure call
That once did love to walk with me
And own thy taste for scenery
That sat for hours by wood and brook   5
And stopt thy curious flowers to look
Were all that met thy artless gaze
Enjoyd thy smiles and won thy praise
O thou that did sincerely love
The cuckoos note and cooing dove   10
And stood in raptures oft to hear
The blackbirds music wild and clear
That chasd sleep from thy lovly eyes
To see the morning lark arise
And made thy evening rambles long   15
To list the crickets chittering ★ song
Thou that on sabbath noons sought bowers
To read away the sultry hours
Were roseys hung the cool to share
With thee a blossom full as fair   20
Oft withering from noons scorching look
And fluttering dropping on thy book
Wispering morals as they fell
What thou ere this hath provd too well
Picturing stories sad and true   25
Beneath thy bright eyes beaming blue
How youth and beauty fades and dyes
The sweetest has the least to prize

How blissfull pleasures fade away
That have the shortest time to stay 30
As suns that blest thy eyes and mine
Are but alowd a day to shine
And fairest days without a cloud
A gloomy evening waits to shroud
So spoke the fading dropping flowers 35
That perishd in thy musing hours
I know not wether thou descryd
But I coud hear them by thy side
But thy warm heart tho easy wrung
Woud not be mellancholy long 40
If such was felt the cheering day
Woud quickly chase their glooms away
For thou sought fancys sweet to look
In every hour and every nook
To thee earth swarmd with lovly things 45
The butterflye with spangld wings
And dragon flye and humble bee
Hummd dreams of paradise to thee
And o thou fairest dearest still
If natures wild mysterious skill 50
Beams that same rapture in thine eye
And left a love that cannot dye
If that fond taste was born to last
Nor vanishd with the summers past
If seasons as they usd to be 55
Still meet a favourd smile with thee
Then thou accept for memorys sake
All I can give or thou canst take
A parted record known to thee
Of what has been no more to be 60
The pleasant past the future sorrow

DEDICATION TO * * * *

The blest today and sad tomorrow—
Descriptions wild of summer walks
By hedges lanes and trackless balks
And many an old familiar scene   65
Were thou has oft my partner been
Were thou enrapt in wild delight
Hast lingerd morning noon and night
And were to fancys rapturd thrill
Thy lovly memory lingers still   70
Thy flowers still bloom and look the while
As tho they witnessd marys smile
The birds still sing thy favourd lays
As tho they sung for marys praise
And bees hum glad and fearless bye   75
As tho their tender friend was nigh
O if with thee those raptures live
Accept the trifle which I give
Tho lost to pleasures witnessd then
Tho parted neer to meet agen   80
My aching heart is surely free
To dedicate its thoughts to thee
Then thou accept and if a smile
Lights on the page thou reads the while
If aught bespeaks those banishd hours   85
Of beauty in thy favourd flowers
Or scenes recall of happy days
That claims as wont thy ready praise
Tho I so long have lost the claim
To joys which wear thy gentle name   90
Tho thy sweet face so long unseen
Seems types of charms that neer hath been
Thy voice so long in silence bound
To me that I forget the sound

And tho thy presence warms my theme   95
Like beauty floating in a dream
Yet I will think that such may be
Tho buried secrets all to me
And if it be as hopes portray
Then will thy smiles like dews of heaven   100
Cheer my lone walks my toils repay
And all I ask be given

Noon

ALL how silent and how still,
Nothing heard but yonder mill;
While the dazzled eye surveys
All around a liquid blaze;
And amid the scorching gleams,   5
If we earnest look it seems
As if crooked bits of glass
Seem'd repeatedly to pass.
O! for a puffing breeze to blow,
But breezes all are strangers now.   10
Not a twig is seen to shake,
Nor the smallest bent* to quake;
From the river's muddy side,
Not a curve is seen to glide;
And no longer in the stream,   15
Watching lies the silver bream,
Forcing from repeated springs,
'Verges in successive rings.'

Bees are faint and cease to hum,
Birds are overpow'r'd and dumb;   20
And no more love's oaten strains,
Sweetly through the air complains;
Rural voices all are mute;
Tuneless lies the pipe and flute;
Shepherds with their panting sheep,   25
In the swaliest★ corner creep;
And from the tormenting heat,
All are wishing to retreat;
Huddled up in grass and flow'rs,
Mowers wait for cooler hours;   30
And the cow-boy seeks the sedge,
Ramping in the woodland hedge,
While his cattle o'er the vales,
Scamper with uplifted tails;
Others not so wild and mad,   35
That can better bear the gad,
Underneath the hedge-row lunge★
Or, if nigh, in waters plunge;

O to see how flow'rs are took!
How it grieves me when I look:—   40
Ragged-robbins once so pink
Now are turn'd as black as ink,
And their leaves being scorch'd so much
Even crumble at the touch.
Drowking★ lies the meadow-sweet   45
Flopping down beneath one's feet;
While to all the flow'rs that blow,
If in open air they grow,

Th'injurious deed alike is done
By the hot relentless sun.   50
E'en the dew is parched up
From the teazle's jointed cup.—
O poor birds where must ye fly,
Now your water-pots are dry?
If ye stay upon the heath   55
Ye'll be chok'd and clamm'd★ to death
Therefore leave the shadeless goss,★
Seek the spring-head lin'd with moss

There your little feet may stand,
Safely printing on the sand;   60
While in full possession, where
Purling eddies ripple clear,
You with ease and plenty blest,
Sip the coolest and the best;
Then away and wet your throats,   65
Cheer me with your warbling notes;
'Twill hot Noon the more revive:
While I wander to contrive
For myself a place as good,
In the middle of a wood;   70
There, aside some mossy bank,
Where the grass in bunches rank
Lifts its down on spindles high,
Shall be where I'll choose to lie;
Fearless of the things that creep,   75
There I'll think and there I'll sleep;
Caring not to stir at all,
Till the dew begins to fall.

What is Life?

AND what is Life? an hour-glass on the run
A mist retreating from the morning sun
  A busy bustling still repeated dream
Its length? A moment's pause, a moment's thought
  And happiness? A bubble on the stream   5
That in the act of siezing shrinks to nought

Vain hopes—what are they? Puffing gales of morn
That of its charms divests the dewy lawn
  And robs each flowret of its gem and dies
A cobweb hiding disappointments thorn   10
  Which stings more keenly thro' the thin disguise

And thou, O trouble? Nothing can suppose,
And sure the Power of Wisdom only knows,
  What need requireth thee.
So free and lib'ral as thy bounty flows,   15
  Some necessary cause must surely be.

And what is death? Is still the cause unfound
The dark mysterious name of horrid sound
  A long and ling'ring sleep the weary crave—
And peace—where can its happiness abound?   20
  No where at all but Heaven and the grave

Then what is Life? When stript of its disguise
   A thing to be desir'd it cannot be
Since every thing that meets our foolish eyes
   Gives proof sufficient of its vanity   25
'Tis but a trial all must undergo
   To teach unthankful mortals how to prize
That happiness vain man's denied to know
   Untill he's call'd to claim it in the skies.

The Harvest Morning

COCKS wake the early morn with many a crow
Loud ticking village clock has counted four
The labouring rustic hears his restless foe
And weary bones and pains complaining sore
Hobbles to fetch his horses from the moor   5
While some are left to teem* the loaded corn
Which night unfinished left agen the door
And bird boy scaring sounds his hollow horn
What busy bustling labouring scene[s] now mark the harvest
   morn

Swift hies the waggon in the field to load   10
And wakes the early morn wi rattling sound
And hogs and geese now throng the dusty road
Grunting and gabbling in contention round
The barley ears that litter on the ground
What printing traces mark the waggons way   15
[What dusty bustling wakens echo round;
How drive the sun's warm beams the mist away;
How labour sweats and toils, and dreads the sultry day!]

The mower scythe now oer his shoulder leans
And wetting* jars a sharp shill* tinkling sound   20
Then swaps again mong corn and rustling beans
And swath by swath flops lengthening oer the ground
[While 'neath some friendly heap, snug shelter'd round
From spoiling sun, lies hid the heart's delight;
And hearty soaks oft hand the bottle round,   25
Their toils pursuing with redoubled might—
Great praise to him be due that brought its birth to light.

Upon the waggon now, with eager bound,
The lusty picker whirls the rustling sheaves;
Or, resting ponderous creaking fork aground,   30
Boastful at once whole shocks of barley heaves:
The loading boy revengeful inly grieves
To find his unmatch'd strength and power decay;
The barley horn his garments interweaves;
Smarting and sweating 'neath the sultry day,   35
With muttering curses stung, he mauls the heaps away.

A motley group the clearing field surround:
Sons of Humanity, oh ne'er deny
The humble gleaner entrance in your ground;
Winter's sad cold, and Poverty are nigh.   40
Grudge not from Providence the scant supply:
You'll never miss it from your ample store.
Who gives denial,—harden'd, hungry hound,—
May never blessings crowd his hated door!
But he shall never lack, that giveth to the poor.   45

Ah, lovely Emma! mingling with the rest,
Thy beauties blooming in low life unseen,
Thy rosy cheeks, thy sweetly swelling breast;
But ill it suits thee in the stubs to glean.

O Poverty! how basely you demean   50
The imprison'd worth your rigid fates confine;
Not fancied charms of an Arcadian queen,
So sweet as Emma's real beauties shine:
Had Fortune blest, sweet girl, this lot had ne'er been thine.

The sun's increasing heat now mounted high,   55
Refreshment must recruit exhausted power;
The waggon stops, the busy tool's thrown by,
And 'neath a shock's enjoy'd the bevering hour. *
The bashful maid, sweet health's engaging flower,
Lingering behind, o'er rake still blushing bends;   60
And when to take the horn fond swains implore,
With feign'd excuses its dislike pretends.
So pass the bevering hours, so Harvest Morning ends.

O Rural Life! what charms thy meanness hide;
What sweet descriptions bards disdain to sing;   65
What loves, what graces on thy plains abide:
Oh, could I soar me on the Muse's wing,
What rifled charms should my researches bring!
Pleas'd would I wander where these charms reside;
Of rural sports and beauties would I sing;   70
Those beauties, Wealth, which you in vain deride,
Beauties of richest bloom, superior to your pride.]

I ALWAYS feel delighted when an object in nature brings up
in ones mind an image of poetry that describes it from some
favourite Author   you have a better oppertunity of consult-
ing books then I have   therefore I will set down a list of
favourite Poems and Poets who went to nature for their
images so that you may consult them and share the feelings

and pleasures which I describe   your favourite Chaucer is
one   Passages in Spencer Cowleys Grasshopper and Swallow
Passages in Shakspear Miltons Allegro and Penseroso and
Parts of Comus the Elizabethian Poets of glorious memory
Gays Shepherds week Greens Spleen Thompsons Seasons
Collins Ode to Evening Dyers Grongar hill and Fleece
Shenstones Schoolmistress Greys Ode to Spring T. Wartons
April Summer Hamlet and Ode to a friend Cowpers Task
Wordsworth Logans Ode to the Cuckoo Langhorns Fables
of Flora Jagos Blackbirds Bloomfields Witchwood Forest
Shooters hill etc with Hurdis's Evening Walk in the village
Curate and many others that may have slipt my memry . . .
the man of taste . . . never sees the daisey without thinking of
Burns and who sees the taller buttercup carpeting the closes
in golden fringe without a remembrance of Chattertons
beautiful mention of it . . . 'The kingcup brasted with the
morning dew'   other flowers crowd my imagination with
their poetic assosiations but I have no room for them   the
clown knows nothing of these pleasures   he knows they are
flowers and just turns an eye on them and plods bye   therefore as I said before to look on nature with a poetic eye
magnifys the pleasure she herself being the very essence and
soul of Poesy

(from a letter to Messrs. Taylor and Hessey, 1822)

Summer Evening

THE sinken sun is takin leave
And sweetly gilds the edge of eve
While purple [clouds] of deepening dye
Huddling hang the western skye

Crows crowd quaking★ over head   5
Hastening to the woods to bed
Cooing sits the lonly dove
Calling home her abscent love
Kirchip kirchip mong the wheat
Partridge distant partridge greet   10
Beckening call to those that roam
Guiding the squandering covey home
Swallows check their rambling flight
And twittering on the chimney light
Round the pond the martins flirt   15
Their snowy breasts bedawbd in dirt
While the mason neath the slates
Each morter bearing bird awaits
Untaught by art each labouring spouse
Curious daubs his hanging house   20
Bats flit by in hood and cowl
Thro the barn hole pops the owl
From the hedge the beetles boom
Heedless buz and drousy hum
Haunting every bushy place   25
Flopping in the labourers face
Now the snail has made his ring
And the moth with snowy wing
Fluttring plays from bent to bent
Bending down with dews besprent   30
Then on resting branches hing★
Stren[g]th to ferry oer the spring
From the haycocks moistend heaps
Frogs now take their vaunting leaps
And along the shaven mead   35
Quickly travelling the[y] proceed
Flying from their speckled sides

Dewdrops bounce as grass divides
[Now the blue fog creeps along,
And the bird's forgot his song:]   40
Flowrets sleep within their hoods
Daisys button into buds
From soiling dew the butter cup
Shuts his golden jewels up
And the Rose and woodbine they   45
Wait again the smiles of day
Neath the willows wavy boughs
Nelly singing milks her cows
While the streamlet bubling bye
Joins in murmuring melody   50

   Now the hedger hides his bill
And with his faggot climbs the hill
Driver Giles wi rumbling joll*
And blind ball* jostles home the roll
Whilom Ralph for doll* to wait   55
Lolls him oer the pasture gate
Swains to fold their sheep begin
Dogs bark loud to drive em in
Plough men from their furrowy seams
Loose the weary fainting team   60
Ball wi cirging* lashes weald
Still so slow to drive afield
Eager blundering from the plough
Wants no wip to drive him now
At the stable door he stands   65
Looking round for friendly hands
To loose the door its fastening pin
Ungear him now and let him in

Round the Yard a thousand ways
The beest in expectation gaze   70
Tugging at the loads of hay
As passing fotherers* hugs away
And hogs wi grumbling deafening noise
Bother round the server boys
And all around a motly troop   75
Anxious claim their suppering up
From the rest a blest release
Gabbling goes the fighting geese
Waddling homward to their bed
In their warm straw litterd shed   80
Nighted by unseen delay
Poking hens then loose their way
Crafty cats now sit to watch
Sparrows fighting on the thatch
Dogs lick their lips and wag their tails   85
When doll brings in the milking pails
With stroaks and pats their welcomd in
And they with looking thanks begin
She dips the milk pail brimming oer
And hides the dish behind the door   90

Prone to mischief boys are met
Gen the heaves* the ladders set
Sly they climb and softly tread
To catch the sparrow on his bed
And kill em O in cruel pride   95
Knocking gen the ladderside
Cursd barbarians pass me by
Come not turks my cottage nigh
Sure my sparrows are my own
Let ye then my birds alone   100

Sparrows come from foes severe
Fearless come yere welcome here
My heart yearns for fates like thine
A sparrows lifes as sweet as mine
To my cottage then resort   105
Much I love your chirping note
Wi my own hands to form a nest
Ill gi ye shelter peace and rest
Trifling are the deed[s] ye do
Grait the pains ye undergo   110
Cruel man woud Justice serve
Their crueltys as they deserve
And justest punishment pursue
And do as they to others do
Ye mourning chirpers fluttering here   115
They woud no doubt be less severe
{Tho ye pluck the farmers wheat} [1]
{Hunger forces all to eat}
Foolhardy clown neer grudge the wheat
Which hunger forces them to eat   120
Your blinded eyes worst foes to you
Neer see the good which sparrows do
Did not the sparrows watching round
Pick up the insect from your grounds
Did not they tend your rising grain   125
You vain might sow—to reap in vain
Thus providence when understood
Her end and aim is doing good
Sends nothing here without its use
Which Ignorance loads with its abuse   130
Thus fools despise the blessing sent
And mocks the givers good intent

[1] Alternative lines in MS.

O god let me the best pursue
As Id have other do to me
Let me the same to others do   135
And learn at least Humanity

   Dark and darker glooms the sky
Sleep gins close the labourers eye
Dobson on his greensward seat
Where neighbours often neighbour meet   140
Of c[r]ops to talk and work in hand
And battle News from foreign land
His last wift* hes puffing out
And Judie putting to the rout
Who gossiping takes great delight   145
To shool* her nitting out at night
Jingling newsing bout the town
Spite o dobs disliking frown
Chattering at her neighbours door
The summons warn her to give oer   150
[Prepar'd to start, she soodles* home,
Her knitting twirling o'er her thumb
As, loth to leave, afraid to stay,
She bawls her story all the way:
The tale so fraught with 'ticing charms,   155
Her apron folded o'er her arms,
She leaves the unfinished tale, in pain,
To end as evening comes again;
And in the cottage gangs* with dread,
To meet old Dobson's timely frown,   160
Who grumbling sits, prepar'd for bed,
While she stands chelping* 'bout the town.]

   Night winds now on sutty wings
In the cotters chimney sings

Sweet I raise my drowsy head   165
Thoughtful stretching on my bed
Listning to the ushering charms
That shakes the Elm trees mossy arms
Till soft slumbers stronger creep
Then rocked by winds I fall to sleep   170

Part of Childhood *or* The Past

THE past it is a magic word
Too beautiful to last
It looks back like a lovely face
Who can forget the past
Theres music in its childhood   5
Thats known in every tongue
Like the music of the wildwood
All chorus to the song

The happy dream the joyous play
The life without a sigh   10
The beauty thoughts can neer pourtray
In those four letters lye
The painters beauty breathing art
The poets speaking pens
Can neer call back a thousand part   15
Of what that word contains

.   .   .   .   .   .

Youth revels at its rising hour
With more then* summer joys
And rapture holds the fairey flower
Which reason soon destroys   20
O sweet the bliss which fancy feigns
To hide the eyes of truth
And beautious still the charm appears
Of faces loved in youth

And spring returns the blooming year   25
Just as it used to be
And joys in youthful smiles appear
To mock the change in me
Each sight leaves memory ill at ease
And stirs an aching bosom   30
To think that seasons sweet as these
With me are out of blossom

The finest summer sinks in shade
The sweetest blossom dies
And age finds every beauty fade   35
That youth esteemed a prize
The play breaks up the blossom dies
And childhood dissapears
For higher dooms ambition tries
And care grows into years   40

But time we often blame him wrong
That rude destroying time
And follow him with sorrows song
When he hath done no crime

Our joys in youth are often sold   45
In follys thoughtless fray
And many feel their hearts grow old
Before their heads are grey

The past there lies in that one word
Joys more then wealth can crown   50
Nor could a million call them back
Though muses wrote them down
The sweetest joys imagined yet
The beautys that surpast
The dearest joys man ever met   55
Are all among the past

I never had much relish for the pastimes of youth   instead
of going out on the green at the town end on Winter sundays
to play football I stuck to my corner stool poreing over a
book   in fact I grew so fond of being alone at last that my
mother was feign to force me into company for the neighbours had assured her mind into the fact that I was no better
then crazy.

I usd to be very fond of fishing and of a sunday morning I
have been out before the sun delving for worms in some old
weed blanketed dunghill and steering off across the wet grain
that overhung the narrow path   and then I used to stoop to
wring my wet trouser bottoms now and then and off agen
beating the heavy drops off the grain with my pole end   I
usd also to be very fond of poking about the hedges in spring
to hunt pootys and I was no less fond of robing the poor birds
nests or searching among the prickly furze on the heath poking
a stick into the rabbit holes and carefuly observing when I
took it out if there was down at the end which was a sign of a
nest with young then in went the arm up to the shoulder and
then fear came upon us that a snake might be conseald in

the hole and then our bloods ran cold within us and startld us
off to other sports

   There is nothing but poetry about the existance of childhood real simple soul moving poetry the laughter and joy
of poetry and not its philosophy   and there is nothing of
poetry about manhood but the reflection and the remembrance of what has been   nothing more   Thus it is that our
play prolonging moon on spring evenings shed a richer lustre
than the midday sun that surrounds us now in manhood for
its poetical sunshine hath left us   it is the same identical sun
and we have learned to know that—for in boyhood every
new day brought a new sun   we knew no better and we was
happy in our ignorance   there is nothing of that new and
refreshing sunshine upon the picture now   it shines from
the heavens upon real matter of fact existances and weary
occupations   The spring of our life—our youth—is the
midsummer of our happiness—our pleasures are then real and
heart stirring—they are but associations afterwards—where
we laughed in childhood at the reality of the enjoyment felt
we only smile in manhood at the reccolections of those enjoyments ... we only feel the joy we possessed   we see the
daisy and love it because it was our first favourite in childhood
when we sat upon the doorstep and cropt its smiling blossoms
by the threshold   we hear the nightingale and are delighted
because it was such a favourite in youth when the romance of
beauty our first love stood in all the simplicity of woman in
the moonlighting valley by our sides to listen the song—when
sunday evenings came like the visits of angels and still the
haunts of its annual visit are in the self same spots the paradise
of our young hearts first extacys—green thickets where the
leaves hide him from all but joys

The Village Boy

FREE from the cottage corner see how wild
The village boys along the pasture hies
With every smell and sound and sight beguiled
That round the prospect meets his wondering eyes
Now stooping eager for the cowslip peeps   5
As though hed get them all—now tired of these
Accross the flaggy brook he eager leaps
For some new flower his happy rapture sees
Now tearing mid the bushes on his knees
On woodland banks for blue bell flowers he creeps   10
And now while looking up among the trees
He spies a nest and down he throws his flowers
And up he climbs with new fed extacies
The happiest object in the summer hours

from The Parish

YOUNG farmer Bigg of this same flimsey class
Wise among fools and with the wise an ass
A farming sprout with more then farmers pride
Struts like the squire and dresses dignified
They call him squire at which his weakness aimd   5
But squires still view him as a fool misnamed
Yet dress and tattle ladys hearts can charm
And hes the choice with madams of the farm
Now with that lady strutting now with this
Braced up in stays as slim as sickly miss   10

Shining at christmass rout and vulgar ball
The favourite spark and rival of them all
And oft hell venture to bemean his pride
Tho bribes and mysterys do their best to hide
Teazing weak maidens with his pert deciet   15
Whose lives are humble but whose looks are sweet
Whose beauty happens to outrival those
With whom the dandy as an equal goes
Thus maids are ruined oft and mothers made
As if bewitchd without a fathers aid   20
Tho nodds and winks and whispers urge a guess
Weakness is bribed and hides its hearts distress
To live dishonoured and to dye unwed
For clowns grow jealous when theyre once misled
Thus pointed fingers brand the passing spark   25
And whispers often guess his deeds are dark
But friends deny and urge that doubts mislead
And prove the youth above so mean a deed
The town agrees and leaves his ways at will
A proud consieted meddling fellow still   30

Churchwardens Constables and Overseers
Makes up the round of Commons and of Peers
With learning just enough to sign a name
And skill sufficient parish rates to frame
And cunning deep enough the poor to cheat   35
This learned body for debatings meet
Tho natures marks are deep that all may scan
A knaves delusions from an honest man
Oppression often mourns the vile abuse
And flyes to justice—deemd of little use   40
Truth that coud once its own redresses seek
Is now deemd nothing and forbid to speek

Drove like an exile king from past renown
Power took its place and keeps it with a frown
And why shoud power or pride betray its trust 45
Is it too old a fashion to be just
Or does self interest inclinations bend
Aye aye the farmer is his worships friend
As parish priest from him he meets his tythes
Punctual as harvest wakes the tinkling scythes 50
Tho often grudgd yet he their hopes to glad
Prays better harvests when the last was bad
And as he deals so honestly with him
It must be malice in the poor or whim
Who seek relief and lay on them the blame 55
And hopless seek it and return the same
Tho many heads the parliment prepare
And each one claims some wisdom for its share
Like midnight with her vapours tis so small
They make but darkness visible with all 60
Their secretary is the Parish Clerk
Whom like a shepherds dog they keep to bark
And gather rates and when the next are due
To cry them oer at church time from his pew
He as their 'Jack of all trades' steady shines 65
Thro thick and thin to sanction their designs
Who apes the part of King and Magistrate
And acts grant seginior of this turkish state
Who votes new laws to those already made
And acts by force when one is disobeyd 70
Having no credit which he fears to loose
He does whatever dirty jobs they chuse
Tasking the pauper labours [   ] to stand
Or clapping on his goods the Parish Brand
Lest he shoud sell them for the want of bread 75

On parish bounty rather pind then fed
Or carrying the parish book from door to door
Claiming fresh taxes from the needy poor
And if ones hunger overcomes his hate
And buys a loaf with what shoud pay the rate　　　80
He instant sets his tyrant laws to work
In heart and deed the essence of a turk
Brings summons for an eighteen penny rate
And gains the praises of the parish state
Or seizes goods and from the burthend clown　　　85
Extorts for extra trouble half a Crown
Himself a beggar that may shortly take
A weekly pittance from the rates they make
But the old proverb suits the subject well
Mount such on horseback and theyll ride to hell　　　90

And weres that lovley maid in days gone bye
The farmers daughter unreserved tho shye
That milked her cows and old songs used to sing
As red and rosey as the lovely spring
Ah these have dwindled to a formal shade　　　95
As pale and bedrid as my ladys maid
Who cannot dare to venture in the street
Some times thro cold at other times for heat
And vulgar eyes to shun and vulgar winds
Shrouded in veils green as their window blinds　　　100
These taught at school their stations to despise
And view old customs with disdainful eyes
Deem all as rude their kindred did of yore
And scorn to toil or foul their fingers more
Prim as the pasteboard figures which they cut　　　105
At school and tastful on the chimney put
They sit before their glasses hour by hour

Or paint unnatural daubs of fruit or flower
Or boasting learning novels beautys quotes
Or aping fashions scream a tune by notes   110
Een poetry in these high polished days
Is oft profained by their dislike or praise
Theyve read the Speaker till without a look
Theyll sing whole pages and lay bye the book
Then sure their judgment must be good indeed   115
When ere they chuse to speak of what they read
To simper tastful some devoted line
As somthing bad or somthing very fine
Thus mincing fine airs misconcieved at school
That pride outherods and compleats the fool   120
Thus housed mid cocks and hens in idle state
Aping at fashions which their betters hate
Affecting high lifes airs to scorn the past
Trying to be somthing makes them nought at last
These are the shadows that supply the place   125
Of famous daughters of the vanished race
And what are these rude names will do them harm
O rather call them 'Ladys of the Farm'
Miss Peevish Scornful once the Village toast
Deemd fair by some and prettyish by most   130
Brought up a lady tho her fathers gain
Depended still on cattle and on grain
She followd shifting fashions and aspired
To the high notions baffled pride desired
And all the profits pigs and poultry made   135
Were gave to Miss for dressing and parade
To visit balls and plays fresh hopes to trace
And try her fortune with a simpering face
And now and then in Londons crowds was shown
To know the world and to the world be known   140

All leisure hours while miss at home sojournd
Past in preparing till new routs returnd
Or tittle tattling oer her shrewd remarks
Of Ladys dresses or attentive sparks
How Mr So and So at such a rout   145
Fixed his eyes on her all the night about
While the good lady seated by his side
Behind her hands her blushes forced to hide
Till conscious Miss in pity she woud say
For the poor lady turnd her face away   150
And young Squire Dandy just returned from france
How he first chose her from the rest to dance
And at the play how such a gent resignd
His seat to her and placed himself behind
How this squire bowd polite at her approach   155
And Lords een nodded as she passd their coach
Thus miss in raptures woud such things recall
And Pa and Ma in raptures heard it all
But when an equal woud his praise declare
And told young madam that her face was fair   160
She might believe the fellows truth the while
And just in sport might condescend to smile
But frownd his further teazing suit to shun
And deemd it rudeness in a farmers son
Thus she went on and visited and drest   165
And deemd things earnest that was spoke in jest
And dreamd at night oer prides uncheckd desires
Of nodding gentlemen and smiling squires
To Gretna green her visions often fled
And rattling coaches lumberd in her head   170
Till hopes grown weary with too long delay
Caught the green sickness* and declined away
And beauty like a garment worse for wear

Fled her pale cheek and left it much too fair
Then she gave up sick visits balls and plays   175
Were whispers turnd to anything but praise
All were thrown bye like an old fashiond song
Where she had playd show woman much too long
And condecended to be kind and plain
And 'mong her equals hoped to find a swain   180
Past follys now were hatful to review
And they were hated by her equals too
Notice from equals vain she tryd to court
Or if they noticed twas but just in sport
At last grown husband mad away she ran   185
Not with Squire Dandy but the servant man

JUST as pride and fashion was creeping out of the citys like
a plague to infest the Village Ralph Wormstall one of the last
of the oppulent Farmers of the Old School flourished in his
popularity whose fame for fat oxen and old Ale got wind
even beyond the out skirts of the county   he was a very rich
plain and superstitious man whose enemys called him 'horse
Shoe Ralph' from a failing he had in believing in witches and
a practice which he indulged in of nailing old horse shoes
about the thresholds of his house and stables to prevail as a spell
against their nightly depredations   he firmly believed that
they rode his sheep trays and cow cribs about the yard on
Winter nights and terrified himself and his horses till he tryed
the above to prevent them which has branded the old farmer
for ever with the name of 'Horse shoe Ralph'   he was a plain
rich old farmer and a good fellow in spite of his nick name and
it was once whispered about the village that he got the Vicar
to conjure some evil spirits in his cellar in a barrel of Ale
which he fancied haunted his stock when his sheep dyed of

the rot one wet season and his swine of the murrain in acorn
time   his enemys vouched it for truth and his friends did
not contradict it but smiled when they heard it and calld it an
'innocent weakness'   be as it woud the Vicar was as superstitious as himself and always quoted the witch of Endor as a
knockdown to unbelievers in witchcraft for he swallowed
every story with the most credulous faith   and because a
farmer once doubted his authority of the 'witch of Endor' as a
proof of their existance he instantly set him down as an Atheist
and declared that he shoud not be buried in the churchyard
if he could help it   the old farmer was very rich but he
never purchased a hunting horse and made it his boast among
Sportsmen of confessing that he never followed a Fox in his
life except to drive him from the henroost and seldom got
astride of a saddle save when he gave old Dobbin a holiday
from the plough to carry his Dame to the Fair to sell her
Stilton cheese   and while the young coxcomb was praising
himself as a 'good shot' he woud confess it as a boast of being
no Sportsman and considered it as a mark of his wisdom for
such ignorance when they talked of their certificates to kill
game he would cock his pipe higher and dryly observe that
his Lordships Gamekeeper always sent a Hare at Christmass
to his old tennants and he shoud be a fool to buy a certificate
to kill one—one Hare a year satisfied his wants and he fancied
one liscence enabled them to shoot no more   he was famous
in Obstinacys and as famous for keeping them   he kept an
old Gun for no other purpose as it woud seem then to hang
among the fire Irons above the kitchen chimney but he found
it useful to shoot sparrows in harvest and fright the Fox from
the hen roost in Winter   he always made it a rule to go to
Market a foot and sold his Eggs and Butter himself as he
thought it a better scheme then trusting to servants and he
even took a pride to crack of his Orchard in good fruit years

and sold both the Apples and Pears as he considered it a shame
to devour any thing in his own house that might be done
without and that woud turn into money   he always sat
at the same table at Harvest suppers with his men and would
never suffer the Oven stone to be opend till the Vicar made
his appearance When they shook hands drank a horn together
as a pledge of thanks for a good harvest and then the supper
was instantly on the table   he always made it a rule to sing
all the songs he knew on that night which were not many and
'When this Old Hat was New' 'Toby Fillpot' and 'Speed the
Plough' were always sung at a heat in quick succession for he
never waited to be asked to sing or stopt to let any one else
till he was done   and he prided himself in knowing 3 such
good Songs for he coud not aspire to much praise in singing
them as he had but a bad voice and readily acknowledgd that
his old friend the Vicar had a better who was fond of a song
tho he always excused himself in a mixed company   and the
old Farmer woud get him off by saying that he did it for the
sake of his 'cloth' tho at the same time he woud urge him to
say 'Chevey Chase' instead of singing it as there coud be
no harm in that which he always readily agreed to   and he
woud listen to any Song except the Vicar of Bray when he
woud instantly get up though his pipe was just lighted and
make excuse to leave the room which never happened at the
old Farmers house where none offered to offend him for
the old farmer woud not laugh at the Vicars expence tho
he was fond of jokes and had two or three 'old Joe Millars' *
which served for all seasons at which none laughd so heartily
as himself   he always had his brown earthern pitcher of his
old ale over a pipe after dinner and he never emptied it
without drinking 'Long life to the King' tho 'peace and
plenty' was his favourite toast in company and he felt it
nessesary to appologize for its frequent use at his sunday dinner

partys (for he never invited friends at another time except the vicar as he had no time to attend to them) by saying 'heres my old health gentlemen "Peace and Plenty" for want of a better' tho he thought at the same time that a better never existed and Vicar woud often confess so when he said it needed no appology   he was a great stickler for 'good old ways' as he called them and woud not suffer any of his family to reach a glass from the cupboard to drink out of when there was no company   and the old Vicar always joined him in believing that the clear horn with its silver rim was far better then glasses   and he seldom was in a passion with the wenches unless they wanted to follow the fashions and never thought his old dame a fool but once when she joind her daughters in thinking that a 'beautiful set of blue China' woud be a better ornament to the cupboard then the old Delf Teapot and white cups and saucers when he declared that they shoud all go without tea the instant they bought them   whenever genteel company made glasses a nessesary appendage to the dinner table he appologized for the use of the old horn to himself by saying it was a gift of his mothers and he coud not discard it   but his wife woud often let out his secret pregudice to glasses by laughing and saying that he never made it a rule to drink healths out of glasses and the old man woud laugh likewise as it gave him an oppertunity of begining up a long praise of his young days when horns and brown earthern ware pitchers were in fashion   and if he was a little warm with liquor he woud lay down his pipe without bidding and sing his old favourite 'When this old hat was new'   the Daughters were often terribly anoyed with his meddlings in their dresses and his staunch canvasings for the old fashion of stays and stomachers and hair hanging down the back instead of being stuck up in combs but the Vicar sided for the girls dresses and thought it 'better for them to dress like

other people then to go otherways' and the old dame woud
finish the vicars story not giving time to say further—'and to
be every bodys laughing stock'   so they wearied his objec-
tions and he suffered them at last to go without stays and
dress up their hair as they pleased tho he never woud agree to
their following the 'Hoggs fashion' as he called it to wear ear
rings so they were always obliged to wear caps in his presence
to hide them   when they talked of new fashons he woud
instantly tell the history of his sunday suit which was a grey
colored coat with hugh★ buttons and a waistcoat of a same
color with large pockets and flaps that hung over his hips big
enough for a modern squires shooting jacket   it was his
'wedding suit' and he seldom had it on without mentioning the
surcumstance and his wife often declared to her guests tho
her husband had been married 40 years that his sunday suit
were as clean and as good as when they were first put on for
the wedding   this always made the old man smile and at the
same time reach his hand to the shelf for the cloathsbrush to
give it a stroke down   his first wish had been to learn them
all to be good Dairey wives by sending them to milk and do
the kitchen work and make the cheese and butter themselves
but his wife told the Vicar it was nothing but a mizardly turn
to save the wages of servants and ruin his daughters by making
them fit for nothing but servants them selves   the old Vicar
woud laugh and say that her 'spark of pride' might be right
enough for what he knew and she over ruled her husband
against sending them to school by reminding him that Moll
Huggings won a nobleman by the accomplishments she learned
there so he let them go with the hopes of making them
ladys   he was very cautious in remembering old customs
and considerd the forgetting one an ill omen   he was always
punctual in having the old bowl of frumitory★ at sheep-
shearing ready in time for the shepherds suppers and never let

the old year go out without warming the old can of ale for the ringers well pepperd with ginger and he woud always have his Yule cake cut at Twelfth night for the Morris dancers to taste of with their beer let the old dame mutter as she might   he always got the fattest goose for Christmass and a couple of the best ducks in the yard for lammass tide and he kept almost every Saint day in the almanack with an additional pitcher after dinner and another pipe at night with the Vicar which he called 'honoring the day' and often remarked as they were all of the same 'cloth' with his good old neighbour (meaning the Vicar for he thought all the saints had been Vicars) they were worth remembering   and as the good old Vicar liked to wet his pipe in a moderate way he never once contradicted the custom or objected to catholics tho King Charles the Martyr and a few others by way of distinction were honoured with a prayer 'for the occasion' and a 'proper lesson' in the Bible read aloud to the family by the Vicar whom the old farmer always complimented as being the best reader in England   tho he did not pretend to much learning himself yet he fancied he coud read a chapter in the Bible with any man except the Vicar and he always made a point of reading one every sunday night aloud to his family and it was generaly from 'Proverbs' for he considered them as the finest parts of Scripture as he said a man coud not be made too wise for the world   the Vicar often tryed in vain to convince him that they aluded to spiritual conserns—for he never coud be beat out of his own way—as he said nothing had two meanings in his mind—so it was no use talking   he professed a little knowledge of books tho his whole acquai[n]tance took up no more then a spare corner on the mantlepiece were the Bible and Mores Almanack stood together which he considered two of the best books that were ever printed   there was the 'Whole duty of man' too which he prized as being a

heir long★ to the family and had belonged to his grandfather
but he had never read it and Elliots Husbandry he had but
he woud not confess that it was of any use to him and only
kept as a family legacy for he used to say that farmers had
done going school now adays and coud farm without Books
at least ought to do   with these lay a heap of pamphlets
among which was the 'History of Jane Shore' 'The King and
the Cobler' 'Johnney Armstrong' and a fragment of an old
book on Cookery with 'Hamlet a tradegy by Will Shakspear
Esqr' but these belongd to the Wife and the last to his daughters
who woud often attempt to read passages of Shakspear on a
winters evening to him a taste which they had brought from
school—but they coud not beat him out of his old favourite
opinion that 'George Barnwell' which his mother took him
to see acted when a boy was a better play than 'Shakspear'
for he always confounded the name with the subject and
thought that Shakspear was the title of a Play the same as
'George Barnwell'   and trying to correct his errors was of
no use for he always stuck to his first opinions of things
wether right or wrong   he prided himself in such obst[i]nacys
by calling those turncoats that were willing to be corrected
out of their old opinions for so he called his errors   they
woud often try to get the Vicar on their side but he only
confessed a dislike for Plays and stopt there   tho the old
Farmer had no knowledge of Poetry—'His music long had
been the plough'—yet like a true Critic he was ever ready
with his opinion in every thing and argued with the Vicars
Latin as stoutly as if he had been at colledge half his life   he
was acquanted with Old Tussers Husbandry and set him
down as the greatest poet on Earth and the Vicar shook his
head in vain quoting scraps from Horace to prove him before
Tusser tho nobody understood a word of the Latin but
himself and the old farmer always fancied that if a man coud

read english they coud read any thing if it was readable   there-
for he always called Horace a fool and his Latin nonsense
because he coud not read it   his Book of Old Tusser had
been 'time out of mind' in his family and the favourite
passages of his father were doubld down still as he left them
at the 'lessons on Thrift' for his father had often called him
'the greatest poet that ever lived' and he deemed the book of
sufficient importance to insert in his 'Will' as a family legacy
which he 'desired might never go out of the family' nor was it
placed on the corner shelf with the rest but carefully kept in
his coffer with a piece of green bays stretched round the
covers to preserve them   the Vicar like his old neighbour
was not much given to books   he neither read much or
pretended to it by talking about it   his chief discourse was
like the old farmers about markets and the weather   and
tho religion seldom shared their conversation the old farmer
and his family were regular churchgoers

> True to the Church no sunday shower
> Kept him at home in that important hour

and he somtimes remarked to the Vicar over their pipes of
his never missing going to church of a Sunday but once in
twenty years and that was when he got his hay out of that
meadow before the 'great July flood' came down for it was a
memorable day with him and he often wondered why Moor
did not put it among the remarkable things in his Almanack
as well as the 'hot Wednesday'   and tho those who lost their
hay blamed him for breaking the sabbath the Old Vicar
excused it and said he was right and preached a sermon in the
right of using urgent nessesitys   the Vicar always stiled his
neighbour a rare churchman and wished the rest of his flock
had attended as regular and heeded as well to his counsels tho
the old farmer thought it no sin to talk about taxes in the

porch or set the Clerk to give notice to the congregation of
new rates under the pulpit as soon as the sermon was ended and
this the Vicar agreed to as right likewise and he was beloved
in the Parish by most as he always prayed for fair or wet
weather as the farmer required . . . the Vicar was somtimes
disposed to be merry and would ramp* with the servant
wenches in hay time about the Cocks and rarely missed
kissing them beneath the missletoe at Christmass which he
considered as a nessesary preface to good luck thro the year for
like his old neighbour he was a stickler for old customs   and
it was whispered about the Village in his young days that he
was fond of women but when ever it was hinted to the farmer's
wife she woud fall in a passion and declare that he was as
honest a man as her husband

Love and Memory

THOU art gone the dark journey
    That leaves no returning
Tis fruitless to mourn thee
    But who can help mourning
To think of the life   5
    That did laugh on thy brow
In the beautiful past
    Left so desolate now

When youth seemed immortal
    So sweet did it weave   10
Heavens haloo around thee
    Earths hopes to decieve

Thou fairest and dearest
   Where many were fair
To my heart thou art nearest   15
   Tho thy name is but there

The nearer the fountain
   More pure the stream flows
And sweeter to fancy
   The bud of the rose   20
And now thourt in heaven
   More pure is the birth
Of thoughts that wake of thee
   Then aught upon earth

As a bud green in spring   25
   As a rose blown in June
Thy beauty looked out
   And departed as soon
Heaven saw thee too fair
   For earths tennants of clay   30
And ere age did thee wrong
   Thou wert summoned away

I know thou art happy
   Why in grief need I be
Yet I am and the more so   35
   To feel its for thee
For thy presence possest
   As thy absence destroyed
The most that I loved
   And the all I enjoyed   40

So I try to seek pleasure
   But vainly I try
Now joys cup is drained
   And hopes fountain is dry
I mix with the living   45
   And what do I see
Only more cause for sorrow
   In loosing of thee

The year has its winter
   As well as its may   50
So the sweetest must leave us
   And the fairest decay
Suns leave us to night
   And their light none may borrow
So joy retreats from us   55
   Oertaken by sorrow

The sun greets the spring
   And the blossom the bee
The grass the blea★ hill
   And the leaf the bare tree   60
But suns nor yet seasons
   As sweet as they be
Shall ever more greet me
   With tidings of thee

The voice of the cuckoo   65
   Is merry at noon
And the song of the nightingale
   Gladdens the moon

But the gayest to day
  May be saddest tomorrow   70
And the loudest in joy
  Sink the deepest in sorrow

But the lovely in death
  And the fairest must die
Fall once and for ever   75
  Like stars from the sky
So in vain do I mourn thee
  I know its in vain
Who could wish thee from joy
  To earths troubles again   80

Yet thy love shed upon me
  Life more then my own
And now thou art from me
  My being is gone
Words know not my grief   85
  Thus without thee to dwell
Yet in one I felt all
  When life bade thee farewell

Valentine—To Mary

THIS visionary theme is thine
From one who loves thee still
Tis writ to thee a valentine
But call it what you will
No more as wont thy beaming eye   5
To violets I compare
Nor talk about the lilys dye
To tell thee thou art fair

The time is past when hopes sweet will
First linked thy heart with mine   10
And the fond muse with simple skill
Chose thee its valentine
Though some may yet their powers employ
To wreath with flowers thy brow
With me thy loves a withered joy   15
With hope thourt nothing now

The all that youths fond spring esteems
Its blossoms plucked in may
Are gone like flowers in summer dreams
And thoughts of yesterday   20
The heavenly dreams of early love
Youths spell has broken there
And left the aching heart to prove
That earth owns nought so fair

Spring flowers were fitting hopes young songs   25
To grace loves earliest vow
But withered ones that autumn wrongs
Are emblems sweetest now
Their perished blooms that once were green
Hopes faded tale can tell   30
Of shadows were a sun hath been
And suit its memory well

Then why should I on such a day
Address a song to thee
When withered hope hath died away   35
And love no more can be

When blinded fate that still destroys
Hath rendered all as vain
And parted from the bosom joys
Twill never meet again   40

The substance of our joys hath been
Their flowers have faded long
But memory keeps the shadow green
And wakes this idle song
Then let esteem a welcome prove   45
That cant its place resign
And friendship takes the place of love
To send a valentine

First Loves Recollections

FIRST love will with the heart remain
When all its hopes are bye
As frail rose blossoms still retain
Their fragrance till they die
And joys first dreams will haunt the mind   5
With shadows whence they sprung
As summer leaves the stems behind
On which springs blossoms hung

Mary I dare not call thee dear
Ive lost that right so long   10
Yet once again I vex thine ear
With memorys idle song

Had time and change neer blotted out
The love of former days
Thou wert the last that I should doubt   15
Of pleasing with my praise

When honied tokens from each tongue
Told with what truth we loved
How rapturous to thy lips I clung
Whilst nought but smiles reproved   20
But now methinks if one kind word
Were whispered in thine ear
Thoudst startle★ like an untamed bird
And blush with wilder fear

How loath to part how fond to meet   25
Had we two used to be
At sunset with what eager feet
I hastened on to thee
Scarce nine days passed us ere we met
In spring nay winter weather   30
Now nine years suns have risen and set
Nor found us once together

Thy face was so familiar grown
Thy self so often nigh
A moments memory when alone   35
Would bring thee to mine eye
But now my very dreams forget
That witching look to trace
Though there thy beauty lingers yet
It wears a strangers face   40

I felt a pride to name thy name
But now that pride hath flown
My words een seem to blush for shame
That own I love thee on
I felt I then thy heart did share   45
Nor urged a binding vow
But much I doubt if thou couldst spare
One word of kindness now

Oh what is now my name to thee
Though once nought seemed so dear   50
Perhaps a jest in hours of glee
To please some idle ear
And yet like counterfeits with me
Impressions linger on
Tho all the gilded finery   55
That passed for truth is gone

Ere the world smiled upon my lays
A sweeter meed was mine
Thy blushing look of ready praise
Was raised at every line   60
But now methinks thy fervent love
Is changed to scorn severe
And songs that other hearts approve
Seem discord to thine ear

When last thy gentle cheek I prest   65
And heard thee feign adieu
I little thought that seeming jest
Would prove a word so true

A fate like this hath oft befell
Even loftier hopes then ours   70
Spring bids full many buds to swell
That neer can grow to flowers

The Cellar Door
A Ballad

BY THE old tavern door on the causway there lay
A hogshead of stingo★ just rolled from a dray
And there stood the blacksmith awaiting a drop
As dry as the cinders that lay in his shop
And there stood the cobler as dry as a bun   5
Almost crackt like a bucket when left in the sun
He's wetted his knife upon pendil★ and hone
Till hed not got a spittle to moisten the stone
So ere he could work though he'd lost the whole day
He must wait the new broach and bemoisten his clay   10

The cellar was empty each barrel was drained
To its dregs—and sir John like a rebel remained
In the street—for removal too powerful and large
For two or three topers to take into charge
Odd zooks said a tinker with bellows to mend   15
Had I strength I would just be for helping a friend
To walk on his legs but a child in the street
Had as much power as he to put John on his feet
Then up came the Blacksmith Sir Barley said he
I should just like to storm your old tower for a spree 20

And my strength for your strength and bar your renown
Id soon try your spirit by cracking your crown
And the cobler he tuckt up his apron and spit
In his hands for a burster but devil a bit
Would he move—so as yet they made nothing of land   25
For there lay the knight like a whale in the sand
Says the tinker if I could but drink of his veins
I should just be as strong and as stubborn again
Push along said the Toper the cellars adry
Theres nothing to moisten the mouth of a fly   30

Says the Host we shall burn out with thirst hes so big
Theres a cag★ of small swipes★ half as sour as a wig
In such like extreems why extreems will come pat
So lets een go and wet all our whistles with that
Says the tinker may I never bottom a chair   35
If I drink of small swipes while Sir Johns lying there
And the blacksmith he threw off his apron and swore
Small swipes should bemoisten his gullet no more
Let it out on the floor for the dry cock-a-roach
And he held up his hammer with threatens to broach   40

Sir John in his castle without leave or law
And suck out his blood with a reed or a straw
Ere hed soak at the swipes—and he turned him to start
Till the host for high treason came down a full quart
Just then passed the dandy and turned up his nose   45
They'd fain had him shoved but he looked at his cloaths—
And nipt his nose closer and twirled his stick round
And simpered tis nuisance to lie on the ground
But bacchus he laughed from the old tavern sign
Saying go on thou shadow and let the sun shine   50

Then again they all tried and the tinker he swore
That the hogshead had grown twice as heavy or more
Nay nay said the toper and reeled as he spoke
Were all getting weak thats the end of the joke
The ploughman came up and cut short his old tune   55
Hallooed 'woi' to his horses and though it was june
Said hed help them an hour ere hed keep them adry
'Well done' said the blacksmith with hopes running high
He moves and by jingos success to the plough''
Aye aye said the cobler well conquer him now   60

The hogshead rolled forward the toper fell back
And the host laughed aloud as his sides they would crack
To see the old tinkers toil make such a gap
In his coat as to rend it from collar to flap
But the tinker he grunted and cried 'fiddle dee'   65
This garment hath been an old tennant with me
And a needle and thread with a little good skill
When Ive leisure will make it stand more weathers still
Then crack went his trunks from the hip to the knee
With his thrusting—no matter for nothing cared he   70

So long as Sir John rolled along to the door
Hes a chip of our block said the blacksmith and swore
And as sure as I live to drive nails in a shoe
He shall have at my cost a full pitcher or two
And the toper he hiccuped which hindered an oath   75
So long as he'd credit he'd pitcher them both
But the host stopt to hint when hed ordered the dray
Sir Barleycorns order was purchase and pay
And now the old knight is iimprisoned and taen
To waste in the tavern mans cellar again   80

And now said the blacksmith let forfeits come first
For the insult swipes offered or his hoops I will burst
Here it is my old heartys—then drink your thirst full
Said the host for the stingo is worth a strong pull
Never fear for your legs if theyre broken to day   85
Winds only blow straws dust and feathers away
But the cask that is full like a jiant he lies
And jiants alone can his spirits capsize
If he lies in the path though a kings coming bye
John Barleycorns mighty and there he will lye   90

Then the toper sat down with a hiccup and felt
If he'd still an odd coin in his pocket to melt
And he made a wry face for his pocket was bare
—But he laughed and danced up 'what old boy are you
    there'
When he felt that a stiver* had got to his knee   95
Through a hole in his fob and right happy was he
Says the tinker Ive brawled till no breath I have got
And not met with twopence to purchase a pot
Says the toper Ive powder to charge a long gun
And a stiver Ive found when I thought I'd got none   100

So by helping a thirsty old friend in his need
Is my duty—take heart thou art welcome indeed
Then the smith with his tools in Sir John made a breach
And the toper he hiccuped and ended his speech
And pulled at the quart* till the snob he declared   105
When he went to drink next that the bottom was bared
No matter for that said the toper and grinned
I had but a soak and neer rested for wind
Thats low said the smith with a look rather vexed
But the quart was a forfiet so pay for the next   110

Then they talked of their skill and their labour till noon
When the sober mans toil was exactly half done
And there the plough lay—people hardly could pass
And the horses let loose pinsored up the short grass
And browsed on the bottle of flags★ lying there   115
By the tinkers old budget★ for mending a chair
The millers horse tyed to the old smithy door
Stood stamping his feet by the flies bitten sore
Awaiting the smith as he wanted a shoe
And he stampt till another fell off and made two   120

Till the miller expecting that all would get loose
Went to seek him and cursed him out right for a goose
But he dipt his dry beak in the mug once or twice
And forgot all his passion and toils in a trice
And the fly bitten horse at the old smithy post   125
Might stamp till his shoes and his legs they were lost
He sung his old songs and forgot his old mill
Blow winds high or low she might rest at her will
And the cobler in spite of his bustle for pelf
Left the shop all the day to take care of itself   130

And the toper who carried his house on his head
No wife to be teazing no bairns to be fed
Would sit out the week or the month or the year
Or a lifetime so long as he'd credit or beer
The ploughman he talked of his skill as divine   135
How he could plough furrows as straight as a line
And the blacksmith he swore had he but the command
He could shoe the kings hunter the best in the land
And the cobler declared was his skill but once seen
He should soon get an order for shoes from the queen   140

But the tinker he swore he could beat them all three
For gi me a pair of old bellows says he
And I'll make them roar out like the wind in a storm
And make them blow fire out of coals hardly warm
The toper said nothing but wished the quart full   145
And swore he could top it all off at a pull
Ha done said the tinker but wit was away
When the bet was to bind him he'd nothing to pay
And thus in the face of lifes sun and shower weather
They drank bragged and sung and got merry together   150

The sun it went down—the last gleam from his brow
Flung a smile of repose on the holiday plough
The glooms they approached and the dews like a rain
Fell thick and hung pearls on the old sorrel mane
Of the horse that the miller had brought to be shod   155
And the morning awoke saw a sight rather odd
For a bit of the halter still hung at the door
Bit through by the horse now at feed on the moor
And the old tinkers budget lay still in the weather
While all kept on singing and drinking together   160

February
A Thaw

THE snow is gone from cottage tops
The thatch moss glows in brighter green
And eves in quick succession drops
Where grinnings icles once hath been

Pit patting wi a pleasant noise   5
In tubs set by the cottage door
And ducks and geese wi happy joys
Douse in the yard pond brimming oer

The sun peeps thro the window pane
Which children mark wi laughing eye   10
And in the wet street steal again
To tell each other spring is nigh
And as young hope the past recalls
In playing groups will often draw
Building beside the sunny walls   15
Their spring-play-huts of sticks or straw

And oft in pleasures dreams they hie
Round homsteads by the village side
Scratting the hedgrow mosses bye
Where painted pooty shells abide   20
Mistaking oft the ivy spray
For leaves that come wi budding spring
And wondering in their search for play
Why birds delay to build and sing

The milkmaid singing leaves her bed   25
As glad as happy thoughts can be
While magpies chatter oer her head
As jocund in the change as she
Her cows around the closes stray
Nor lingering wait the foddering boy   30
Tossing the molehills in their play
And staring round in frolic joy

Ploughmen go whistling to their toils
And yoke again the rested plough
And mingling oer the mellow soils   35
Boys' shouts and whips are noising now
The shepherd now is often seen
By warm banks oer his work to bend
Or oer a gate or stile to lean
Chattering to a passing friend   40

Odd hive bees fancying winter oer
And dreaming in their combs of spring
Creeps on the slab beside their door
And strokes its legs upon its wing
While wild ones half asleep are humming   45
Round snowdrop bells a feeble note
And pigions coo of summer coming
Picking their feathers on the cote

The barking dogs by lane and wood
Drive sheep afield from foddering ground   50
And eccho in her summer mood
Briskly mocks the cheery sound
The flocks as from a prison broke
Shake their wet fleeces in the sun
While following fast a misty smoke   55
Reeks from the moist grass as they run

Nor more behind his masters heels
The dog creeps oer his winter pace
But cocks his tail and oer the fields
Runs many a wild and random chase   60

Following in spite of chiding calls
The startld cat wi harmless glee
Scaring her up the weed green walls
Or mossy mottld apple tree

As crows from morning perches flye 65
He barks and follows them in vain
Een larks will catch his nimble eye
And off he starts and barks again
Wi breathless haste and blinded guess
Oft following where the hare hath gone 70
Forgetting in his joys excess
His frolic puppy days are done

The gossips saunter in the sun
As at the spring from door to door
Of matters in the village done 75
And secret newsings mutterd oer
Young girls when they each other meet
Will stand their tales of love to tell
While going on errands down the street
Or fetching water from the well 80

A calm of pleasure listens round
And almost whispers winter bye
While fancy dreams of summer sounds
And quiet rapture fills the eye
The sun beams on the hedges lye 85
The south wind murmurs summer soft
And maids hang out white cloaths to dry
Around the eldern skirted croft

Each barns green thatch reeks in the sun
Its mate the happy sparrow calls   90
And as nest building spring begun
Peeps in the holes about the walls
The wren a* sunny side the stack
Wi short tail ever on the strunt
Cockd gadding up above his back   95
Again for dancing gnats will hunt

The gladdend swine bolt from the sty
And round the yard in freedom run
Or stretching in their slumbers lye
Beside the cottage in the sun   100
The young horse whinneys to its mate
And sickens from the threshers door
Rubbing the straw yards banded gate
Longing for freedom on the moor

Hens leave their roosts wi cackling calls   105
To see the barn door free from snow
And cocks flye up the mossy walls
To clap their spangld wings and crow
About the steeples sunny top
The jackdaw flocks resemble spring   110
And in the stone archd windows pop
Wi summer noise and wanton wing

The small birds think their wants are oer
To see the snow hills fret again
And from the barns chaff litterd door   115
Betake them to the greening plain

The woodmans robin startles coy
Nor longer at his elbow comes
To peck wi hungers eager joy
Mong mossy stulps* the litterd crumbs   120

Neath hedge and walls that screen the wind
The gnats for play will flock together
And een poor flyes odd hopes will find
To venture in the mocking weather
From out their hiding holes again   125
Wi feeble pace they often creep
Along the sun warmd window pane
Like dreaming things that walk in sleep

The mavis thrush wi wild delight
Upon the orchards dripping tree   130
Mutters to see the day so bright
Spring scraps of young hopes poesy
And oft dame stops her burring wheel
To hear the robins note once more
That tutles while he pecks his meal   135
From sweet briar hips beside the door

The hedghog from its hollow root
Sees the wood moss clear of snow
And hunts each hedge for fallen fruit
Crab hip and winter bitten sloe   140
And oft when checkd by sudden fears
As shepherd dog his haunt espies
He rolls up in a ball of spears
And all his barking rage defies

Thus nature of the spring will dream   145
While south winds thaw but soon again
Frost breaths upon the stiffening stream
And numbs it into ice—the plain
Soon wears its merry garb of white
And icicles that fret at noon   150
Will eke their icy tails at night
Beneath the chilly stars and moon

Nature soon sickens of her joys
And all is sad and dumb again
Save merry shouts of sliding boys   155
About the frozen furrowd plain
The foddering boy forgets his song
And silent goes wi folded arms
And croodling★ shepherds bend along
Crouching to the whizzing storms   160

Valentine Eve

YOUNG girls grow eager as the day retires
And smile and whisper round their cottage fires
Listning for noises in the dusky street
For tinkling latches and for passing feet
The prophecys of coming joys to hark   5
Of wandering lovers stealing thro' the dark
Dropping their valentines at beautys door
With hearts and darts and love knots littered oer
'Aye' said a gossip by a neighbours hearth

While the young girls popt up in tittering mirth   10
To hear the door creak with heart jumping signs
And footsteps hastening bye and valentines
Drop rustling on the floor—'aye aye' she said
As they kept back and smiled oer what they read
'Your fine love letters might be worth your smiles   15
If 'stead of coming from some creeping giles
Rich lovers sent them as it once befell
To one young maiden I remember well
Tho Madam Meers now lives at Oakley Hall
With coach and four and footmen at her call   20
Her father was none else than farmer Ling
And she plain Kate before she wore a ring
Tho I began about the valentine
The starting subject I'll awhile resign
But hear with patience and ye'll quickly learn   25
For I'll haste on and take it up in turn
    When the poor irish from their country rove
And like scotch cattle throng the road in droves
To seek the profits which the harvest brings
At that same season to old farmer Lings   30
A stranger came but not of foreign blood
He spoke plain english and his looks was good
And hired himself for toil the season thro
At any jobs the harvest had to do
And tho he seemed as merry as the clowns★   35
He neer was noisey like such vulgar lowns★
And when he heard them urge a vulgar joke
At passing maids he neither laughd nor spoke
But while he saw the blush their rudeness made
His manners seemed their freedom to upbraid   40
For hed turn round a moment from his toil
And say 'good morning' and would kindly smile

Tho dressed like them in jacket russet brown
His ways betrayed him better than a clown
And many a guess from rumours whispers fell   45
And gossips daily had new tales to tell
Some said he once had been a wealthy man
And from a bankrupts painful ruin ran
Others with far worse causes marked his flight
And taxed him with a forgers name out right   50
And tho he heard such whispers passing bye
Hed laugh but never stop to question why
Nor seemed offended think whatere he would
But always seemed to be in merry mood
Bad as folks thought him I was well aware   55
That he by one at least was welcome there
Who always mid their noisey idle prate
Would silent stand and that was rosey Kate
She seemed bewitched with his good mannered ways
And never spoke about him but to praise   60
She was the youngest daughter fair and gay
As flowers that open in the dews of May
Loves heart neer trembled at a sweeter face
When health and beauty courted its embrace
Nor lived a merrier girl beneath the sun   65
For romp and play when labours work was done
Wild as a Doe that overleapt the park
She'd laugh and play oer evenings games till dark
All noise and stir like an ill sitting hen
But shoy* and timid in the sight of men   70
Her friends neer dreamed of what all else might see
His ways was plain as the 'cross row'* to me
When ere he caught her in her dissabille
Washing or aught—she ran as lovers will
Up stairs as quickly as she could from sight   75

To seek her glass and put her garments right
Anxious to meet him in her best attire
As he the more might love her and admire
And once at eve as we the cows did wait
He leaned beside her on the stackyard gate   80
And smiled and whispered as she stooped adown
To pull some burdocks from her sweeping gown
'Mary theres one whose thoughts when your away
'Always cling with you full as close as they
'Who hopes yet fears his growing love to name   85
'Lest you should throw it from you just the same'
She coloured like the fire and turned aside
But I saw quickly what her heart would hide
And up and told her when she milked at night
That be the harvest stranger who he might   90
A winning tongue neath toils disguise was hid
That knew more manners then our farmers did
She laughd and said 'Aye so you love him then
But as for her shed no regard for men'
Tho such denials kept the secret worse   95
I took no heed but sanctioned her discourse
And when she dressed to walk on harvest eves
Spending an hour to glean among the sheaves
Things were to others eyes full often seen
That she'd more errands then the one to glean   100
She always followed in the strangers toil
Who oft would stop to wet his hook and smile
And loose when none percieved from out his hand
Some wheat ears now and then upon the land
And oft when running from a sudden shower   105
Or leaving off to take their beavering hour
He always from the rest would linger last
To leave a smile and greet her as he past

All that had any sense to use their eyes
Might easy guess beneath the thin disguise   110
Like to the burr★ about the moon at night
It seems to covert★ but still leaves it light
And sure enough he was a handsome swain
One any maiden had been proud to gain
Een I have often envied Kittys place   115
And felt the heartache at his smiling face
For when I passed him he would always smile
And often took my milk pail oer a stile
Jeering us both of sweethearts in our play
Tho nothing but in good behaviours way   120
He said to me—yet without shame I say't
I thought myself as fine a wench as Kate
Dark as the strangers mystery were his ways
He wandered round the field on sabbath days
And left to vulgar minds the noisey town   125
Nor made a partner of a fellow clown
Tracing the wood tracks over grown with moss
Or with heath rabbits winding thro the goss★
And oft neath blackthorn shadows by the brook
Was seen by shepherds musing oer a book   130
And in his button holes was always seen
Wild flowers—that in his rambles he would glean
Folks often marvelled at each seeming whim
What we thought weeds seemed best of flowers with
    him
The ragged robin by the runnel brinks   135
Seemed in his eye much finer flowers then pinks
And tall wild woad that lifts its spirey★ tops
By stone pits—nay een briony and hops
He would from hedges in a poesy★ bind
And leave the woodbine and the rose behind   140

All wondered at his ways and some believed
The man was crazed but rumour gets decieved
   When busy harvest to its end had come
And childern ran to hollow* 'harvest home'
Bawling half hidden neath each green ash bough   145
For cross plumb skittles* out of fashion now
Kate was the queen upon that merry night
And rode upon the waggon drest in white
The stranger half looked up to see her stand
And smiling called her 'queen of fairey land'   150
That harvest supper we had morts* of fun
And Farmer Sparks was there a neighbours son
He was her fathers choice who dreamed of gain
And talked of marriage as he would of grain
He vainly tryed young Kittys smiles to share   155
And next her without bidding took his chair
Full oft with gracious simperings looking up
To drink to Kitty oer the silver cup
While she but with a careless look replied
Or turned like one that would not heed aside   160
But if the stranger gazed above his horn
She smiled as lovely as a may day morn
Soon as the racket and the fun began
Young Farmer Sparks up from the table ran
To act the crane* and poked the room about   165
Breaking the pipes and putting candles out
While wenches squealed and old dames fainted pale
Quickly recovering with an horn of ale
The stranger seemed to shun the rude uproar
And Kate slove* with him to the kitchen door   170
I sat on thorns the live long night about
For fear their ways would blab the secret out
And had aught met the fathers jealous sight

Farewell to fun and frolic for the night
But all went right and naught was seen or done   175
To spoil the acting or to damp the fun
The old man smoked his pipe and drank his ale
And laughed most hearty at each sport and tale
On the next day for Kate a gloomy day
The harvest labourers took their parting pay   180
And the young stranger with a downcast eye
Turned round to Kate and bade us both 'good bye'
Soon as he went she ran with eager feet
Up stairs to see him vanish down the street
I heard the creeking casement open thrown   185
And knew full well what she neer cared to own
For her swelled eyes their secrets badly kept
When she came down they told me she had wept
Twas harmless sorrows did her bosom move
And theres no sin nor shame to weep for love   190
Sometimes she seemed as sad and sometimes gay
But never more appeared so fond of play
Lone pastimes now did leisure hours engage
Dull as a tame bird wonted to the cage
She seemed to be while time unheeding went   195
Nor left a hope to ease her discontent
    At length the postman with his wind pluft* cheek
That brought the news and letters once a week
Some mornings after valentine was bye
Came in and gan his parcel to untie   200
Her sisters bustled up and smiling thought
That he some lovers valentines had brought
But hopes with them was quickly out of date
Soon as they found the letter was for Kate
Poor wench her colour came and went away   205
Now red as crimson then as pale as may

The old man thought it farmer Sparkes's son
That sent the thing and felt his wishes won
Laying his pipe down he began to joke
And clapt her on the shoulder as he spoke   210
'Have at him wench thats all I have to tell
'And bonny Kate will sell her beauty well
'For he's got money wench as well as love
'To make your ring sit easy as a glove'
But when he found the postmark and the seal   215
Did different notions to his own reveal
He let the mystery undisturbed remain
And turned his chair and took his pipe again
Her sisters bit their lips in silent spite
And could not keep their envy out of sight   220
To think that bonny Kate above them all
Who never in her life had seen a ball
Nor spent an hour to curl her parted hair
Nor of her beauty seemed to have one care
That romped about at play and joined in toil   225
While they would sit and not a finger soil
Should be thus noticed—but they urged a doubt
And muttered some low bred ingenious★ lout
Had sent the thing and said with louder voice
'Be who he will he wears a vulgar choice'   230
And tho they might clowns valentines condemn
Een they were welcome when they came to them
For Sawney★ Sparks and each young farmer guest
Was little better then a clown at best
Be who he might it made their bosoms ache   235
And worse when time unriddled their mistake
   Kate had no pride about her she was free
As any maiden in the world could be
And while her sisters dressed in muslin gowns

And scorned on holidays to talk with clowns   240
She seemed to wear no better dress then I
Yet won a look from every passer bye
And some that passed would mutter praises loud
'Theres a sweet face' which never made her proud
She made all equals—used een beggars well   245
And all of Kate had some kind things to tell
    When summer eves the first come swallows meet
As Kate and I were looking down the street
These little summer visitors to view
Marking how lowley and how swift they flew   250
We heard the bustle of a coach and four
Race the lane dust and hurry towards the door
The yard dog never barked nor made a fuss
But dropt his tail and stopt to gaze with us
Een the old geese were silent at the sight   255
And in amazement half forgot their spite
The noisey childern in the streets at play
Picked up their tops and taws★ and sneaked away
And Kate half startled sneaked and hurried in
While wonder heaved her bosom to her chin   260
And well it might for twas the very same
Man that at harvest as a reaper came
The same that sent her at the valentine
The clever letter that was wrote so fine
Old women that had muttered round the town   265
And called the stranger by worse names then clown
Peeped out and dropped their courtseys★ to the
    coach
And mixed in groups to question its approach
Fine as he was soon as he came in view
I knew his face and so did Kitty too   270
Who overcame turned white as was the wall

And almost fainted but he stopt the fall
And kept her in his arms with fondling pain
Till the fresh rose came to her face again
Her father gaped and wondered at the throng 275
And bowed and chattered wether right or wrong
Guessing that love was what the stranger meant
The coach was plenty to buy his consent
And thinking Kate had made her fortune now
He bustled up and gan to scrape and bow 280
And bade Kate welcome in her noble guest
With wine and ale the oldest and the best
But he was not to be by flattery fed
He only smiled and never turned his head
I want no formal welcomes keep your place 285
Old man he said—But why that blushing face
My bonny Kate I left thee fond and true
And wish to find thee as I used to do
Smiling and free as on each harvest morn
When I as labourer reaped thy fathers corn 290
I travelled in disguise alone to find
The native undisguise of womans mind
Theyre easy coyed* to take a golden bait
And love in mockery—but my bonny Kate
I found in thee a heart I wished to prove 295
Who ignorant of wealth was caught by love
Then shrink not if thy heart is still sincere
Nor blush nor startle with confounding fear
To see thy mother at this finery awed
And father bow and christen me 'my lord' 300
No honours and no titled names are mine
But all I have plain love and wealth is thine
Tho I have grown above thy fathers toil
In reaping corn and ploughing up the soil

Yet that fond love my Kitty showed to me   305
Was neer a moment from my memory
Thy beauty would bewitch a world with love
And I've returned thy worth and vows to prove
Ive came as promised for thee many a mile
Then bid me welcome with thy usual smile   310
Reach not sweet Kate the silver cup for me
But bring the horn toil often drank to thee
And thus he said but how can words of mine
Relate a speech that he told oer so fine
However there they sat the night about   315
And drank the old brown pitcher nearly out
Kate often smiled but yet was still and shoy
And the old man got down right drunk for joy
Who often reached across his elbow chair
To gain the whisper of his daughters ear   320
Muttering when ere the stranger turned his head
His urgent wishes in her looks to wed
Fingers in vain were shook to keep him still
He een got wilder in his head strong will
'—A good receipt neer makes a bargain wrong   325
'So Kate says he burn nothing with your tongue'
And drank her health anew—the strangers eye
Looked smiling at him but made no reply
When morning came Kate gave her hearts consent
The coach was ordered and to church they went   330
Before the sun the old man bustled up
And gave his blessing oer the silver cup
At the glad closing of that happy day
The stranger drove his blooming bride away
She left her presents for the cake and tea   335
Leaving old gossips in the highest glee
While he with gifts the ringers did regale

Who rung his praises both with bells and ale
And tho she promised me a handsome gown
When eer she married be he gent or clown   340
No wonder that her memory was away
I quite excused her breaking it that day
  He was no lord tho he was full as great
A country squire with a vast estate
In the most trifling things she had her ends   345
And ere she'd gone a twelvemonth from her friends
She wished once more to see us all again
And as indulgence to her lonely pain
They in their coach and four came shining down
To rent a dwelling near her native town   350
And Oakley Hall that tops old Cromwells hill
He took to please and occupys it still
A fine old place with ivy round the porch
That long had stood as empty as a church
Folks say it had a Cromwells castle been   355
And in the walls still cannon holes are seen
There they in happiness and luxury live
And share the all lifes pleasure has to give
Sometimes they visit at their own estate
And yearly drive to London with the great   360
  Whenever I have errands from the town
To seek the hall she gives me many a crown
Making me welcome in plain friendly ways
And often laughs about our younger days
Hark thats the clock well I must up and roam   365
My man no doubt sits waiting me at home
Wholl scold and say by sitting here till nine
That Im an old fool keeping Valentine
So good night all' and hastening from her seat
She sought her clogs and clocked adown the street   370

The girls were glad twas done—and in her place
The happy cat leapt up and cleaned her face
While crickets that had been unheard so long
Seemed as she stopt to start a merrier song

I DO NOT know how to class the venemous animals further
then by the vulgar notion of putting toads common snakes
black snakes—calld by the Peasantry Vipers—Newts (often
calld eatherns) and a nimble scaly looking newt-like thing
about the heaths calld Swifts* by the furze kidders* and cow
keepers   all these we posses in troublsome quantitys all of
which is reckond poisonous by the common people tho a
many daring people has provd that the common snake is not
for I have seen men with whom I have workd in the fields
take them up and snatch them out of joint as they calld it in a
moment so that when they was thrown down they coud not
stir but lay and dyd   others will take them up in one hand
and hold the other agen that double pointed fang which
they put out in a threatning manner when pursued and which
is erroniously calld their sting and when it touches the hand it
appears utterly harmless and turns again as weak as an horse
hair   yet still they are calld poisonous and dreaded by many
people and I myself cannot divest my feelings of their first
impressions tho I have been convincd to the contrary   we
have them about us in great quantitys   they even come in
the village and breed in the dunghills in farm yards and
harbour in old walls   they are fond of lying rolld up like a
whipthong in the sun   they seem to be always jealous of
danger as they never lye far from their hiding places and
retreat in a moment at the least noise or sound of approaching
feet   they lay a great number of eggs white and large   the
shell is a skinny substance and full of a glutiness matter like

the white in birds eggs   they hang together by hundreds as if
strung on a string   they lay them on the south side of old
dunghills were the heat of the sun and the dung together
hatches them   when they first leave the shells they are no
thicker then a worsted needle or bodkin   they nimble ★
about after the old snakes and if they are in danger the old
ones open their mouths and the young dissapear down their
throats in a moment till the danger is over and then they
come out and run about as usual   I have not seen this myself
but I am as certain of it as if I had because I have heard it
told so often by those that did when I have been pilling ★ bark
in the woods in oaking time   I have seen snakes creeping
half errect by the sides of the fallen oaks that were pilld
putting their darting horse hair like tongue every now and
then to the tree and I was a long while ere I could make out
what they were doing but I made it out at last in my mind
that they were catching flyes that were attracted there in
great quantitys to the moister of the sap just after the bark
had been ripd off   this I have observd many times and I think
if it were examind they have a sticky moister at the end of
those double ended fangs that appear like a bit of wailbone
split at the end or a double horse hair which attaches to the
flye as soon as touchd like bird lime and I think this is the use
for which nature designd their mistaken stings   the motion
was so quick that the prey which it seizd coud not be percievd
when taken but I have not the least doubt that such was its
object   people talk about the Watersnake but I cannot
believe otherwise then that the water and land snake are one
tho I have killd snakes by the water in meadows of a different
and more deep color then those I have found in the fields   the
water snake will swallow very large frogs   I have often
known them to be ripd out of their bellys by those who have
skind the snake to wear the skin round their hats which is

reckond as a charm against the headach and is often tryd but with what success I am not able to say . . . when the french prisoners were at Norman cross Barracks it was a very common thing among the people of the villages round to go in the fens a snake catching and carry home large sticks of them strung like eels on osiers which the French men woud readily buy as an article of very palatable food . . . the common snake is very fond of milk and it often makes its way into a dairy by a mouse hole or some other entrance to sip the cream—in the fens (were they are as numerous as flies) they will creep up the milk pails that are set to cool at the door of an evening by 3 or four together

PASTORAL poems are full of nothing but the old thread bare epithets of 'sweet singing cuckoo' 'love lorn nightingale' 'fond turtles' 'sparkling brooks' 'green meadows' 'leafy woods' etc etc these make up the creation of Pastoral and descriptive poesy and every thing else is reckond low and vulgar in fact they are too rustic for the fashionable or prevailing system of ryhme till some bold inovating genius rises with a real love for nature and then they will no doubt be considerd as great beautys which they really are

THE encouragment my first Volume met with lifted me up into heartsome feelings and ryhming was continually with me night and day I began the Village Minstrel a long while before attempting to describe my own feelings and love for rural objects and I then began in good earnest with it after the trial of my first poems was made and compleated it was little time but I was still unsatisfied with it and am now and often feel sorry that I did not withold it a little longer for revision the reason why I dislike it is that it does not

describe the feelings of a ryhming peasant strongly or localy
enough

I BELIEVE that the habits of the land rail or landrake and the
Quail are little known   in fact I know but little of them
myself but that little is at your pleasure   Were is the school
boy that has not heard that mysterious noise which comes
with the spring in the grass and green corn   I have followd it
for hours and all to no purpose   it seemd like a spirit that
mockd my folly in running after it   the noise it makes is a
low craking very much like that of a Drake from whence I
suppose it got the name of Landrake   I never started it up
when a boy but I have often seen it flye since   about two
years ago while I was walking in a neighbours homstead we
heard one of these landrails in his wheat   we hunted down
the land and accidentily as it were we started it up   it seemd
to flye very awkard and its long legs hung down as if they
were broken   it was just at dewfall in the evening   it flew
towards the street instead of the field and popt into a chamber
window that happend to be open when a cat seizd and killd
it   it was somthing like the quail but smaller and very
slender with no tail scarcly and rather long legs   it was of a
brown color   they lay like the quail and partridge upon the
ground in the corn and grass   they make no nest but scrat
a hole in the ground and lay a great number of eggs   My
mother found a landrails nest once while weeding wheat with
seventeen eggs and they were not sat on   they were short
eggs made in the form of the partridges not much unlike the
color of the plovers   I imagine the young run with 'the
shells on their heads' as they say by partridges and plovers
for most of these ground hatchd birds do . . . the year before
last I was helping to carry yaumd★ beans which are shorn
with a hook instead of being mown with a scythe and

stoukd in shoves like wheat   as I was throwing one of these
shoves* upon the waggon somthing ran from under it
very quick and squatted about the land   I mistook it at first
for a rat as it hastend bye me and struck at it with my fork
but on percieving my mistake I stoopd down to catch it   it
awkardly took wing and settld in a border of bush   I found
it was a landrail by its legs dangling down as it flew

The Wren

WHY is the cuckoos melody preferred
And nightingales sick song so madly praised
In poets ryhmes is there no other bird
In natures minstrelsy that hath not raised
Ones heart to extacy and mirth as well   5
I judge not how anothers taste is caught
With mine theres other birds that bear the bell
Whose song hath crowds of happy memorys brought
Such is the robin singing in the dell
And little wren that many a time hath sought   10
Shelter from showers in huts where I did dwell
At early spring the tenant of the plain
Keeping my sheep and still they come to tell
The happy storys of the past again

The Fern Owls Nest

THE weary woodman rocking* home beneath
His tightly banded faggot wonders oft
While crossing over the furze crowded heath
To hear the fern owls cry that whews* aloft

In circling whirls and often by his head 5
Wizzes as quick as thought and ill at rest
As through the rustling ling★ with heavy tread
He goes nor heeds he tramples near its nest
That underneath the furze or squatting thorn
Lies hidden on the ground and teazing round 10
That lonely spot she wakes her jarring noise
To the unheeding waste till mottled morn
Fills the red east with daylights coming sounds
And the heaths echoes mocks the herding boys

Sand Martin

THOU hermit haunter of the lonely glen
And common wild and heath—the desolate face
Of rude waste landscapes far away from men
Where frequent quarrys give thee dwelling place
With strangest taste and labour undeterred 5
Drilling small holes along the quarrys side
More like the haunts of vermin than a bird
And seldom by the nesting boy descried
Ive seen thee far away from all thy tribe
Flirting★ about the unfrequented sky 10
And felt a feeling that I cant describe
Of lone seclusion and a hermit joy
To see thee circle round nor go beyond
That lone heath and its melancholly pond

The March Nightingale

N o w sallow* catkins once all downy white
Turn like the sunshine into golden light
The rocking clown leans oer the spinny rail
In admiration at the sunny sight
The while the blackcap doth his ears assail   5
With a rich and such an early song
He stops his own and thinks the nightingale
Hath of her monthly reckoning counted wrong
'Sweet jug jug jug' comes loud upon his ear
Those sounds that unto may by right belong   10
Yet on the awthorn scarce a leaf appears
How can it be—spell struck the wandering boy
Listens again—again the sound he hears
And mocks it in his song for very joy

T H E Gloworm is a sort of catterpillar insect and thousands
of them may be seen on Casterton Cowpasture on a summer
night   they appear as if a drop of dew hung at their tails
which had been set on fire by the fairys for the purpose of a
lanthorn—and I have often gathered them up and put them
into leaves to see if they shone by daylight but when day came
they were nothing but a little dark looking insect apparently
half dead and as it were shrivelled up   another insect is as
commonly and infact more commonly known as the gloworm among the common people because it frequents their
houses shining very brilliantly anights like liquid silver and
leaving if touchd part of its shining qualities littered about
where it crawled   this when seen by day light is a red long

insect with a great quantity of legs and therebye called the
forty legged worm

The Nightingales Nest

Up this green woodland ride lets softly rove
And list the nightingale—she dwelleth here
Hush let the wood gate softly clap—for fear
The noise may drive her from her home of love   ·
For here Ive heard her many a merry year   5
At morn and eve nay all the live long day
As though she lived on song—this very spot
Just where that old mans beard all wildly trails
Rude arbours oer the road and stops the way
And where that child its blue bell flowers hath got   10
Laughing and creeping through the mossy rails
There have I hunted like a very boy
Creeping on hands and knees through matted thorns
To find her nest and see her feed her young
And vainly did I many hours employ   15
All seemed as hidden as a thought unborn
And where these crimping★ fern leaves ramp★ among
The hazels under boughs—Ive nestled down
And watched her while she sung—and her renown
Hath made me marvel that so famed a bird   20
Should have no better dress than russet brown
Her wings would tremble in her extacy
And feathers stand on end as twere with joy
And mouth wide open to release her heart
Of its out sobbing songs—the happiest part   25
Of summers fame she shared—for so to me
Did happy fancys shapen her employ

But if I touched a bush or scarcely stirred
All in a moment stopt—I watched in vain
The timid bird had left the hazel bush   30
And at a distance hid to sing again
Lost in a wilderness of listening leaves
Rich extacy would pour its luscious strain
Till envy spurred the emulating thrush
To start less wild and scarce inferior songs   35
For cares with him for half the year remain
To damp the ardour of his speckled breast
While nightingales to summers life belongs
And naked trees and winters nipping wrongs
Are strangers to her music and her rest   40
Her joys are evergreen her world is wide
—Hark there she is as usual lets be hush
For in this black thorn clump if rightly guest
Her curious house is hidden—part aside
These hazel branches in a gentle way   45
And stoop right cautious neath the rustling boughs
For we will have another search to-day
And hunt this fern strown thorn clump round and round
And where this seeded wood grass idly bows
Well wade right through—it is a likely nook   50
In such like spots and often on the ground
Theyll build where rude boys never think to look
Aye as I live her secret nest is here
Upon this white thorn stulp—Ive searched about
For hours in vain—there put that bramble bye   55
Nay trample on its branches and get near
—How subtle is the bird she started out
And raised a plaintive note of danger nigh
Ere we were past the brambles and now near
Her nest she sudden stops—as choaking fear   60

That might betray her home so even now
Well leave it as we found it—safetys guard
Of pathless solitude shall keep it still
See there shes sitting on the old oak bough
Mute in her fears our presence doth retard   65
Her joys and doubt turns all her rapture chill
  Sing on sweet bird may no worse hap befall
Thy visions then the fear that now decieves
We will not plunder music of its dower
Nor turn this spot of happiness to thrall   70
For melody seems hid in every flower
That blossoms near thy home—these harebells all
Seems bowing with the beautiful in song
And gaping cuckoo with its spotted leaves
Seems blushing of the singing it has heard   75
How curious is the nest no other bird
Uses such loose materials or weaves
Their dwellings in such spots—dead oaken leaves
Are placed without and velvet moss within
And little scraps of grass—and scant and spare   80
Of what seems scarce materials down and hair
For from mans haunts she seemeth nought to win
Yet nature is the builder and contrives
Homes for her childerns comfort even here
Where solitudes deciples spend their lives   85
Unseen save when a wanderer passes near
That loves such pleasant places—deep adown
The nest is made an hermits mossy cell
Snug lie her curious eggs in number five
Of deadened green or rather olive brown   90
And the old prickly thorn bush guards them well
And here well leave them still unknown to wrong
As the old woodlands legacy of song

April 21 [1825]

I WENT to take my walk to day and heard the Nightingale for
the first time this season in Royce wood just at the town
end   we may now be assured that the summer is nigh at
hand   you asked me a long while back to procure you a
Nightingales nest and eggs and I have try'd every season
since to find if the bird nesting boys have ever taken one out
but I have not been able to procure one—when I was a boy I
usd to be very curious to watch the nightingale to find her
nest and to observe her color and size for I had heard many
odd tales about her and I often observed her habits and found
her nest so I shall be able to give you a pretty faithful history—
she is a plain bird somthing like the hedge sparrow in shape
and the female Firetail or Redstart in color but more slender
then the former and of a redder brown or scorchd color then
the latter   the breast of the male or female is spotted like a
young Robin and the feathers on the rump and on parts of
the wings are of a fox red or burnt umber hue   one of them
is of a darker brown then the other but I know not wether
it be the male or female   they generally seek the same
solitudes which they haunted last season and these are the
black thorn clumps and thickets about the woods and
spinneys   they sit in the water grains* of oaks or on a twig
of hazel and sing their varied songs with short intervals both
in the night and day time and sing in one as common as the
other   I have watchd them often at their song   their
mouths is open very wide and their feathers are ruffled up and
their wings trembling as if in extacy   the superstition of
laying their throats on a sharp thorn is a foolish absurdity but
it is not the only one ascribed to the nightingale   they make
a large nest of the old oak leaves that strew the ground in
woods and green moss and line it with hair and some times a

little fine witherd grass or whool   it is a very deep nest and is
generaly placed on the root or stulp of a black or white thorn
somtimes a little height up the bush and often on the ground

they lay 5 eggs about the size of the woodlarks or larger
and of a deep olive brown without spot or tinge of another
color   their eggs have a very odd appearance and are unlike
any other birds in the county   when they have young their
song ceases and they make an odd burring noise as if calling
their young to their food   they are very jealous of intrusions
on their privacy when they have young and if one goes in
their haunts at that time they make a great chirping and
burring and will almost perch close to you noising and chirping as if to fight you away   at first one assails you and after
it has been chirping about you a while the other approaches
to join it but as soon as you get a little distance from the
haunts they leave you and are still   when if you return they
resume their former chirping and continue fluttering about
you among the branches till you leave them agen to their
privacy

their nest[s] are very difficult to find   indeed it is a hopless
task to hunt for them as they are seldom found but by
accident being hidden among the tall weeds that surround the
roots and cover the woods undisturbed recesses   when I was
a boy I found three nests one season and all were found by
chance in crossing the woods hunting the nests of other birds—
the Red breast frequently builds on the ground under the
shelter of a knoll or stulp and its nest is often taken for that
of the nightingales but it is easily distinguished from it as the
robins is built with dead grass and moss on the out side while
the Nightingale never forgets her dead oak leaves and this is
so peculiar to her taste that I never saw a nest of theirs without
them nor are they used by any other bird for their nests—

The Ravens Nest

UPON the collar of an hugh★ old oak
Year after year boys mark a curious nest
Of twigs made up a faggot near in size
And boys to reach it try all sorts of schemes
But not a twig to reach with hand or foot   5
Sprouts from the pillared trunk and as to try
To swarm the massy bulk tis all in vain
They scarce one effort make to hitch them up
But down they sluther★ soon as ere they try
So long hath been their dwelling there—old men   10
When passing bye will laugh and tell the ways
They had when boys to climb that very tree
And as it so would seem that very nest
That ne'er was missing from that self same spot
A single year in all their memorys   15
And they will say that the two birds are now
The very birds that owned the dwelling then
Some think it strange yet certaintys at loss
And cannot contradict it so they pass
As old birds living the woods patriarchs   20
Old as the oldest men so famed and known
That even men will thirst into the fame
Of boys at get at schemes that now and then
May captivate a young one from the tree
With iron claums★ and bands adventuring up   25
The mealy trunk or else by waggon ropes
Slung over the hugh grains and so drawn up
By those at bottom one assends secure
With foot rope stirruped—still a perrilous way
So perrilous that one and only one   30

In memorys of the oldest men was known
To wear★ his boldness to intentions end
And reach the ravens nest—and thence acchieved
A theme that wonder treasured for supprise
By every cottage hearth the village through   35
Not yet forgot though other darers come
With daring times that scale the steeples top
And tye their kerchiefs to the weather cock
As trophys that the dangerous deed was done
Yet even now in these adventureous days   40
No one is bold enough to dare the way
Up the old monstrous oak where every spring
Finds the two ancient birds at their old task
Repairing the hugh nest—where still they live
Through changes winds and storms and are secure 45
And like a landmark in the chronicles
Of village memorys treasured up yet lives
The hugh old oak that wears the ravens nest

Crows in Spring

THE crow will tumble up and down
   At the first sight of spring
And in old trees around the town
   Brush winter from its wing

No longer flapping far away   5
   To naked fen they flye
Chill fare as on a winters day
   But field and valleys nigh

Where swains are stirring out to plough
    And woods are just at hand   10
They seek the uplands sunny brow
    And strut from land to land

And often flap their sooty wings
    And sturt to neighboring tree
And seems to try all ways to sing   15
    And almost speaks in glee

The ploughman hears and turns his head
    Above to wonder why
And there a new nest nearly made
    Proclaims the winter bye   20

The schoolboy free from winters frown
    That rests on every stile
In wonder sets his basket down
    To start his happy toil

[The Badger]

THE badger grunting on his woodland track
With shaggy hide and sharp nose scrowed* with black
Roots in the bushes and the woods and makes
A great hugh burrow in the ferns and brakes
With nose on ground he runs a awkard pace   5
And anything will beat him in the race
The shepherds dog will run him to his den
Followed and hooted by the dogs and men

The woodman when the hunting comes about
Go round at night to stop the foxes out   10
And hurrying through the bushes ferns and brakes
Nor sees the many hol[e]s the badger makes
And often through the bushes to the chin
Breaks the old holes and tumbles headlong in

When midnight comes a host of dogs and men   15
Go out and track the badger to his den
And put a sack within the hole and lye
Till the old grunting badger passes bye
He comes and hears they let the strongest loose
The old fox hears the noise and drops the goose 20
The poacher shoots and hurrys from the cry
And the old hare half wounded buzzes bye
They get a forked stick to bear him down
. And clapt the dogs and bore him to the town
And bait him all the day with many dogs   25
And laugh and shout and fright the scampering hogs
He runs along and bites at all he meets
They shout and hollo down the noisey streets

He turns about to face the loud uproar
And drives the rebels to their very doors   30
The frequent stone is hurled where ere they go
When badgers fight and every ones a foe
The dogs are clapt and urged to join the fray
The badger turns and drives them all away
Though scarcly half as big dimute* and small   35
He fights with dogs for hours and beats them all
The heavy mastiff savage in the fray
Lies down and licks his feet and turns away

The bull dog knows his match and waxes cold
The badger grins and never leaves his hold   40
He drive[s] the crowd and follows at their heels
And bites them through the drunkard swears and reels

The frighted women takes the boys away
The blackguard laughs and hurrys on the fray
He tries to reach the woods a awkard race   45
But sticks and cudgels quickly stop the chace
He turns agen and drives the noisey crowd
And beats the many dogs in noises loud
He drives away and beats them every one
And then they loose them all and set them on   50
He falls as dead and kicked by boys and men
Then starts and grins and drives the crowd agen
Till kicked and torn and beaten out he lies
And leaves his hold and cackles groans and dies

Some keep a baited badger tame as hog   55
And tame him till he follows like the dog
They urge him on like dogs and show fair play
He beats and scarcely wounded goes away
Lapt up as if asleep he scorns to fly
And siezes any dog that ventures nigh   60
Clapt like a dog he never bites the men
But worrys dogs and hurrys to his den
They let him out and turn a harrow down
And there he fights the host of all the town
He licks the patting hand and trys to play   65
And never trys to bite or run away
And runs away from noise in hollow trees
Burnt by the boys to get a swarm of bees

[The Marten]

THE martin cat long shaged of courage good
Of weazle shape a dweller in the wood
With badger hair long shagged and darting eyes
And lower then the common cat in size
Small head and running on the stoop   5
Snuffing the ground and hind parts shouldered up
He keeps one track and hides in lonely shade
Where print of human foot is scarcely made
Save when the woods are cut the beaten track
The woodmans dog will snuff cock tailed and black   10
Red legged and spotted over either eye
Snuffs barks and scrats the lice and passes bye
The great brown horned owl looks down below
And sees the shaggy martin come and go

The martin hurrys through the woodland gaps   15
And poachers shoot and make his skin for caps
When any woodman come and pass the place
He looks at dogs and scarcely mends his pace
And gipseys often and birdnesting boys
Look in the hole and hear a hissing noise   20
They climb the tree such noise they never heard
And think the great owl is a foreign bird
When the grey owl her young ones cloathed in down
Seizes the boldest boy and drives him down
They try agen and pelt * to start the fray   25
The grey owl comes and drives them all away
And leaves the martin twisting round his den
Left free from boys and dogs and noise and men

[The Fox]

THE shepherd on his journey heard when nigh
His dog among the bushes barking high
The ploughman ran and gave a hearty shout
He found a weary fox and beat him out
The ploughman laughed and would have ploughed him in   5
But the old shepherd took him for the skin
He lay upon the furrow stretched and dead
The old dog lay and licked the wounds that bled
The ploughman beat him till his ribs would crack
And then the shepherd slung him at his back   10
And when he rested to his dogs supprise
The old fox started from his dead disguise
And while the dog lay panting in the sedge
He up and snapt and bolted through the hedge

He scampered [to] the bushes far away   15
The shepherd call[ed] the ploughman [to] the fray
The ploughman wished he had a gun to shoot
The old dog barked and followed the pursuit
The shepherd through [sic] his hook and tottered past
The ploughman ran but none could go so fast   20
The woodman threw his faggot from the way
And ceased to chop and wondered at the fray
But when he saw the dog and heard the cry
He threw his hatchet but the fox was bye
The shepherd broke his hook and lost the skin   25
He found a badger hole and bolted in
They tryed to dig but safe from dangers way
He lived to chase the hounds another day

[The Hedgehog]

THE hedgehog hides beneath the rotten hedge
And makes a great round nest of grass and sedge
Or in a bush or in a hollow tree
And many often stoops and say they see
Him roll and fill his prickles full of crab[s]   5
And creep away and where the magpie dabs ★
His wing at muddy dyke in aged root
He makes a nest and fills it full of fruit
On the hedge bottom hunts for crabs and sloes
And whistles like a cricket as he goes   10
It rolls up like a ball or shapeless hog
When gipseys hunt it with their noisey dogs
Ive seen it in their camps they call it sweet
Though black and bitter and unsavoury meat

But they who hunt the field for rotten meat   15
And wash in muddy dyke and call it sweat [sic]
And eat what dogs refuse where ere they dwell
Care little either for the taste or smell
They say they milk the cows and when they lye
Nibble their fleshy teats and make them dry   20
But they whove seen the small head like a hog
Rolled up to meet the savage of a dog
With mouth scarce big enough to hold a straw
Will neer believe what no one ever saw
But still they hunt the hedges all about   25
And shepherd dogs are trained to hunt them out
They hurl with savage force the stick and stone
And no one cares and still the strife goes on

Hares at Play

THE birds are gone to bed the cows are still
And sheep lie panting on each old mole hill
And underneath the willows grey green bough
Like toil a resting—lies the fallow plough
The timid hares throw daylights fears away   5
On the lanes road to dust and dance and play
Then dabble in the grain by nought deterred
To lick the dewfall from the barleys beard
Then out they sturt again and round the hill
Like happy thoughts dance squat and loiter still   10
Till milking maidens in the early morn
Gingle their yokes and start them in the corn
Through well known beaten paths each nimbling hare
Sturts quick as fear—and seeks its hidden lair

[The Robin]

AGAIN the robin waxes tame
And ventures pitys crumbs to claim
Picking the trifles off the snow
Which dames on purpose daily throw
And perching on the window sill   5
Where memory recolecting still
Knows the last winters broken pane
And there he hops and peeps again

THE little Robin has begun his summer song in good
earnest   he was singing at my chamber window this morning
almost before daylight as he has done all the week and at
night fall he comes regularly to his old plumb tree and starts

it again   there is a plaintive sweetness in the song of this
bird that I am very fond of   it may be calld an eternal song
for it is heard at intervals all the year round and in the Autumn
when the leaves are all fled from the trees there is a mellancholy sweetness in it that is very touching to my feelings   the
Robin is one of the most familiar birds that a village landscape
posseses and it is no less beloved for even childern leave its
nest unmolested but the Wren and the Martin are held in the
like veneration with a many people who will not suffer their
nests to be destroyed   the Robin seems to be fond of the
company and haunts of man   it builds its nest close to his
cottage in the hovel or out house thatch or behind the woodbine or sweet briar in the garden wall nor does it seem to care
to make any secret of its dwelling were its only enemy is
the cat to whom its confidence of saftey often falls a prey   and
it seeks its food by his door on the dunghill or on the garden
beds nay it will even settle on the gardeners spade when he
is at work to watch the worm that he throws up and un-
bears and in winter it will venture into the house for food
and become as tame as a chicken   we had one that usd to
come in at a broken pane in the window three winters
together   I always knew it to be our old visitor by a white
scar on one of the wings which might have been an old wound
made by some cat   it grew so tame that it woud perch on
ones finger and take the crumbs out of the hand   it was very
much startled at the cat at first but after a time it took little
notice of her further then always contriving to keep out of
her way   it woud never stay in the house at night tho it
woud attempt to perch on the chair spindles and clean its
bill and ruffle its feathers and put its head under its wing as if
it had made up its mind to stay but somthing or other
always molested it when it suddenly sought its old broken
pane and departed . . . it has been a common notion among

heedless observers that the robin frequents no were but in villages but this is an erronious one for it is found in the deepest solitudes of woods and forrests were it lives on insects and builds its nest on the roots or stools* of the underwood or under a hanging bank by a dykeside which is often mistook for that of the nightingales   I have often observed its fondness for man even here for in summer I scarcely cross a wood but a Robin suddenly falls in my path to court my acquaintance and pay me a visit were it hops and flutters about as if pleased to see me and in winter it is the woodmans companion for the whole day and the whole season . . . It is not commonly known that the Robin is a very quarrelsome bird   it is not only at frequent warfare with its own species but attacks boldly every other small bird that comes in its way and is gennerally the conqeror   I have seen it chase the house sparrow which tho a very pert bird never ventures to fight it   hedge sparrows linnets and finches that crowd the barn doors in winter never stands against its authority but flyes from its interferences and acknowledge it the cock of the walk and he always seems to consider the right of the yard as his own

A Sunday with Shepherds and Herdboys

THE shepherds and the herding swains
Keep their sabbath on the plains
They know no difference in its cares
Save that all toil has ceasd but theirs
For them the church bells vainly call   5
Fields are their church and house and all

Till night returns their homward track
When soon morns suns recall them back
Yet still they love the days repose
And feel its peace as sweet as those 10
That have their freedom—and maid and clown
To walk the meadows or the town
Theyll lye and catch the humming sound
That comes from steeples shining round
Enjoying in the service time 15
The happy bells delightfull chime
And oft they sit on rising ground
To view the landscap spreading round
Swimming from the following eye
In greens and stems of every dye 20
Oer wood and vale and fens smooth lap
Like a richly colourd map
Square platts★ of clover red and white
Scented wi summers warm delight
And sinkfoil★ of a fresher stain 25
And different greens of varied grain
Wheat spindles bursted into ear
And browning faintly—grasses sere
In swathy seed pods dryd by heat
Rustling when brushd by passing feet 30
And beans and peas of deadening green
And corn lands ribbon stripes between
And checkering★ villages that lye
Like light spots in a deeper sky
And woods black greens that crowding spots 35
The lanscape in leaf bearing grots
Were mingling hid lapt up to lare★
The panting fox lyes cooly there
And willow grove that idly sweas★

And checkering shines mid other trees   40
As if the mornings misty vail
Yet lingerd in their shadows pale
While from the village foliage pops
The popples* tapering to their tops
That in the blue sky thinly wires   45
Like so many leafy spires
Thus the shepherd as he lyes
Were the heaths furze swellings rise
Dreams oer the scene in visions sweet
Stretching from his hawthorn seat   50
And passes many an hour away
Thus musing on the sabbath day
And from the fields theyll often steal
The green peas for a sunday meal
When near* a farmers on the lurch   55
Safe nodding oer their books a church*
Or on their benches by the door
Telling their market profits oer
And in snug nooks their huts beside
The gipsey blazes they provide   60
Braking the rotten* from the trees
While some sit round to shell the peas
Or pick from hedges pilferd wood
To boil on props their stolen food
Sitting on stones or heaps of brakes*   65
Each of the wild repast partakes
Telling to pass the hours along
Tales that to fitter days belong
While one within his scrip* contains
A shatterd bibles thumbd remains   70
On whose blank leaf wi pious care
A host of names is scribbld there

Names by whom twas once possest
Or those in kindred bonds carresst
Childern for generations back   75
That doubtful memory should not lack
Their dates tis there wi care applyd
When they were born and when they dyd
From sire to son link after link
All scribbld wi unsparing ink   80
This he will oft pull out and read
That takes of sunday better heed
Then they who laugh at tale and jest
And oft hell read it to the rest
Whose ignorance in weary mood   85
Pays more regard to robin hood
And giant blue beard and such tales
That live like flowers in rural vales
Natural as last years faded blooms
Anew wi the fresh season comes   90
So these old tales from old to young
Take root and blossom were they sprung
Till age and winter bids them wane
Then fond youth takes them up again
The herdboys anxious after play   95
Find sports to pass the time away
Fishing for struttles★ in the brooks
Wi thread for lines and pins for hooks
And stripping neath the willow shade
In warm and muddy ponds to bathe   100
And pelting wi unerring eye
The heedless swallows starting bye
Oft breaking boughs from trees to kill
The nest of whasps beside a hill
Till one gets stung then they resort   105

And follow to less dangerous sport
Leaving to chance their sheep and cows
To thread the brakes and forest boughs
And scare the squirrels lively joys
Wi stones and sticks and shouting noise   110
That sat wi in its secret place
Upon its tale to clean its face
When found they shout wi joy to see
It hurly burly round a tree
And as they turn in sight again   115
It peeps and squats behind a grain
And oft theyll cut up sticks to trye
The holes were badgers darkly lye
Looking for foot mark prints about
The fresh moulds not long rooted out   120
And peep in burroes newly done
Were rabbits from their noses run
Were oft in terrors wild affright
They spy and startle at the sight
Rolld like a whip thong round and round   125
Asleep upon the sunny ground
A snake that wakens at their play
And starts as full of fear as they
And knewt* shapd swifts that nimbly pass
And rustle in the brown heath grass   130
From these in terrors fears they haste
And seek agen the scrubby waste
Were grass is pincered short by sheep
And venom creatures rarely creep
Playing at taw in sheep beat tracks   135
Or leap frog oer each others backs
Or hump oer hills wi thime oergrown
Or mere marks ancient mossey stone

Or run down hollows in the plain
Were steps are cut to climb again   140
Stone pits that years have clothd in green
And slopd in narrow vales between
Or historys uncrowded ground
A cromwell trench or roman mound
Thus will the boys wi makeshift joy   145
Their toil taskd sabbath hours employ
And feed on fancys sweet as they
That in the town at freedom play
And pinder* too is peeping round
To find a tennant for his pound   150
Heedless of rest or parsons prayers
He seldom to the church repairs
But thinks religion hath its due
In paying yearly for his pew
Soon as the morn puts night away   155
And hastening on her mantle grey
Before one sunbeam oer the ground
Spindles its light and shadow round
He's oer the fields as soon as morn
To see what stock are in the corn   160
And find what chances sheep may win
Thro gaps the gipseys pilfer thin
Or if theyve found a restless way
By rubbing at a loosend tray*
Or neighing colt that trys to catch   165
A gate at night left off the latch
By traveller seeking home in haste
Or the clown by fancys chasd
That lasting while he made a stand
Opens each gate wi fearful hand   170
Fearing a minute to remain

And put it on the latch again
And cows who often wi their thorns
Toss from the gaps the stuffing thorns
These like a fox upon the watch   175
He in the morning tryes to catch
And drives them to the pound for pay
Carless about the sabbath day

The Shepherds Fire

ON THE rude heath yclad in furze and ling
And oddling thorns that thick and prickly grows
Shielding the shepherd when the rude wind blows
And boys that sit right merry in a ring
Round fires upon a molehill toasting sloes   5
And crabs★ that froth and frizzle on the coals
Loud is the gabble and the laughter loud
The rabbits scarce dare peep from out their holes
Unwont to mix with such a noisey crowd
Some run to eke the fire—while many a cloud   10
Of smoke curls up some on their haunches squat
With mouth for bellows puffing till it flares
Or if that fail one fans his napless hat
And when the feast is done they squabble for their shares

I WAS fond of books before I began to write poetry   these
were such that chance came at—6py Pamphlets that are in
the possesion of every door calling hawker and found on
every book stall at fairs and markets whose titles are as
familiar with every one as his own name   shall I repeat

some of them   'Little red riding hood' 'Valentine and Orson'
'Jack and the Jiant' 'Tom Long the carrier' 'The king and the
cobler' 'Sawney Bear' 'The seven Sleepers' 'Tom Hicka-
thrift' 'Johnny Armstrong' 'Idle Laurence' . . 'Robin Hoods
garland' 'old mother Shipton and old Nixons Prophecys'
'History of Gotham' and many others   shall I go on   no
these have memorys as common as Prayer Books and Psalters
with the peasantry   such were the books that delighted
me and I savd all the pence I got to buy them for they were
the whole world of literature to me and I knew of no other   I
carried them in my pocket and read them at my leisure and
they was the never weary food of winter evenings ere Milton
Shakspear and Thompson had ever existed in my memory
and I feel a love for them still   nay I cannot help fancying
now that cock robin babes in the wood mother hubbard and
her cat etc etc are real poetry in all its native simplicity and as
it shoud be   I know I am foolish enough to have fancys
different from others and childhood is a strong spell over my
feelings but I think so on and cannot help it

PLEASURES are of two kinds   one arises from cultivation of
the mind and are enjoyed only by the few and these are the
most lasting and least liable to change   the more common
pleasures are found by the many like beautiful weeds in a
wilderness   they are of natural growth and tho very beautiful
to the eye are only annuals   these may be called the pleasures
of the passions and belong only to the different stages of our
existance   the pleasures of youth are enjoyd in youth
only   after that the very reccolections of their sweetness
sour and embitter the infirmitys of manhood that can no
longer enjoy them

Labours Leisure

O FOR the feelings and the carless health
That found me toiling in the fields—the joy
I felt at eve with not a wish for wealth
When labour done and in the hedge put bye
My delving spade—I homeward used to hie   5
With thoughts of books I often read by stealth
Beneath the blackthorn clumps at dinners hour
It urged my weary feet with eager speed
To hasten home where winter fires did shower
Scant light now felt as beautiful indeed   10
Where bending oer my knees I used to read
With earnest heed all books that had the power
To give me joy in most delicious ways
And rest my spirits after weary days

Aye when long summer showers lets labour win   15
Sweet leisure—how I used to mark with joy
The south grow black and blacker to the eye
Till the rain came and pessed* me to the skin
No matter anxious happiness was bye
With her refreshing pictures through the rain   20
Carless of bowering bush and sheltering tree
I homeward hied to feed on books again
For they were then a very feast to me
The simplest things were sweetest melody
And nothing met my eager taste in vain   25
And thus to read I often wished for rain
Such leisure fancys fed my lowly lot
Possessing nothing and still wanting not

It is an happiness that simplest hearts
Find their own joy in what they undertake   30
That nature like the seasons so imparts
That every mind its own home comfort makes
That be our dwelling in the fields or woods
No matter custom so endears the scenes
We feel in lonliness sweet company   35
And many a varied pleasure intervenes
Which the wide world unnoting passes bye
Pursuing what delights it varied joy
Thus happiness is with us joys succeed
Spontaneous everywhere like summer weeds   40
The cheerful commoners of every spot
Blessing the highest and the lowliest lot

The Woodman

Now evening comes and from the new laid hedge
The woodman rustles in his leathern guise
Hiding in dyke ylined with brustling★ sedge
His bill and mattock from thefts meddling eyes
And in his wallets storing many a pledge   5
Of flowers and boughs from early sprouting trees
And painted pootys from the ivied hedge
About its mossy roots his boys to please
Who wait with merry joy his coming home
Anticipating presents such as these   10
Gained far afield where they nor night nor morn
Find no school leisure long enough to go
Where flowers but rarely from their stalks are torn
And birds scarce loose★ a nest the season through

I CAME to the flood washd mead or stream and then my
tackle was eagerly fastend on and my heart woud thrill with
hopes of success as I saw a sizable gudgeon twinkle round the
glossy pebbles or a fish leap after a flye or a floating somthing
on the deeper water   were is the angler that hath not felt
these delights in his young days and were is an angler that
doth not feel taken with their memory when he is old?

Angling

ANGLING has pleasures that are much enjoyed
By tasteful minds of nature never cloyed
In pleasant solitudes where winding floods
Pass level meadows of oerhanging woods
Verged with tall reeds that rustle in the wind   5
A soothing music in the anglers mind
A rush right complasant that ever bows
Obesceience to the stream that laughs below
He feels delighted into quiet praise
And sweet the pictures that the mind essays   10
While gentle whispers on the southern wind
Brings health and quiet to the anglers mind
Smooth as the gentle river whirls along
And sweet as memory of some happy song

The morn is still and balmy all that moves   15
The trees are south gales which the angler loves
That stirs the waving grass in idle whirls
And flush the cheeks and fan the jetty curls
Of milking maidens at their morns employ
Who sing and wake the dewy fields to joy   20

The sun just rising large and round and dim
Keeps creeping up oer the flat meadows brim
As rising from the ground to run its race
Till up it mounts and shows a ruddy face
Now is the time the angler leaves his dreams   25
In anxious movements for the silent streams
Frighting the heron from its morning toil
First at the river watching after spoil

Now with the rivers brink he winds his way
For a choice place to spend the quiet day   30
Marking its banks how varied things appear
Now cloathed in trees and bushes and now clear
While steep the bank climbs from the waters edge
Then almost choaked with rushes flags and sedge
Then flat and level to the very brink   35
Tracked deep by cattle running there to drink
At length he finds a spot half shade half sun
That scarcely curves to show the waters run
Still clear and smooth quick he his line unlaps
While fish leap up and loud the water claps   40
Which fills his mind with pleasures of supprise
That in the deep hole some old monster lies

Right cautious now his strongest line to take
Lest some hugh monster should his tackle break
Then half impatient with a cautious throw   45
He swings his line into the depths below
The water rat hid in the shivering reeds
That feeds upon the slime and water weeds
Nibbling their grassy leaves with crizzling* sound
Plunges below and makes his fancys bound   50

With expectations joy—down goes the book
In which glad leisure might for pleasure look
And up he grasps the angle in his hand
In readiness the expected prize to land
While tip toe hope gives expectations dream   55
Bright as the sunshine sleeping on the stream

None but true anglers feel that gush of joy
That flushes in the patient minds employ
While expectation upon tip toe sees
The float just wave it cannot be a breeze   60
For not a waver oer the waters pass
Warm with the joyous day and smooth as glass
Now stronger moved it dances round then stops
Then bobs again and in a moment drops
Beneath the water—he with joys elate   65
Pulls and his rod bends double with the weight
True was his skill in hopes expecting dream
And up he draws a flat and curving bream
That scarcely landed from the tackle drops
And on the bank half thronged in sedges stops   70

Now sport the waterflyes with tiny wings
A dancing crowd imprinting little rings
And the rich light the suns young splendours throw
Is by the very pebbles caught below
Behind the leaning tree he stoops to lean   75
And soon the stirring float again is seen
A larger yet from out its ambush shoots
Hid underneath the old trees cranking* roots
The float now shakes and quickens his delight
Then bobs a moment and is out of sight   80

Which scarce secured down goes the cork again
And still a finer pants upon the plain
And bounds and flounces mid the new mown hay
And luck but ceases with the closing day

I HAVE often wondered how birds nests escape injuries which
are built upon the ground   I have found larks nests in an
old cart rut grassed over and pettichaps close on the edge of a
horse track in a narrow lane where two carts could not pass
and two oxen would even have difficulty in doing so but yet
I never found a nest destroyed   providence was their pro-
tector   and on the cow pasture I have often seen an hungry
ox sturt its head on one side making a snufting noise and
cease eating for a minute or two and then turn in another
direction and on going to see what it turned from I have
started up the old bird and found its nest often by this sign

The nightingales nest in the orchard hedge was composed
without side of dead maple leaves and some oak leaves and
lined within with withered grass and a few fragments of
oak leaves

Long tailed titmouse and Chaffinch and red cap make a
most beautiful outside to their nests of grey lichen   linnets
and hedgsparrows make a loose ruff outside of coarse green
moss wool and roots   the first are like the freestone fabrics of
finished ellegance   the latter like the rough plain walls of a
husbandman's cottage yet equally warm and comfortable
within   Pinks* use cowhair and some feathers for their
inside hangings   redcaps get thistle down   hedge sparrows

use wool and cowhair intermixed   linnets use wool and cowhair and the furze linnet uses rabbit down   these four sorts
of birds never (I think) are known to use horse hair while
yellow hammers ground larks yellow wagtails and skylarks
never use wool or cowhair but on the contrary small roots
and horse hair and this universaly   bulfinches make a slight
nest of sticks and small roots very shallow   whitethroats use
dead hariff* stalks linked with cobwebs and lined with fine
roots and horsehair

Shadows of Taste

TASTE with as many hues doth hearts engage
As leaves and flowers do upon natures page
Not mind alone the instinctive mood declares
But birds and flowers and insects are its heirs
Taste is their joyous heritage and they   5
All choose for joy in a peculiar way
Birds own it in the various spots they chuse
Some live content in low grass gemmed with dews
The yellow hammer like a tasteful guest
Neath picturesque green molehills makes a nest   10
Where oft the shepherd with unlearned ken
Finds strange eggs scribbled as with ink and pen
He looks with wonder on the learned marks
And calls them in his memory writing larks
Birds bolder winged on bushes love to be   15
While some choose cradles on the highest tree
There rocked by winds they feel no moods of fear
But joy their birthright lives for ever near
And the bold eagle which mans fear enshrouds

Would could he lodge it house upon the clouds   20
While little wrens mistrusting none that come
In each low hovel meet a sheltered home
Flowers in the wisdom of creative choice
Seem blest with feeling and a silent voice
Some on the barren roads delight to bloom   25
And others haunt the melancholly tomb
Where death the blight of all finds summers hours
Too kind to miss him with her host of flowers
Some flourish in the sun and some the shade
Who almost in his morning smiles would fade   30
These in leaf darkened woods right timid stray
And in its green night smile their lives away
Others in water live and scarcely seem
To peep their little flowers above the stream
While water lilies in their glories come   35
And spread green isles of beauty round their home
All share the summers glory and its good
And taste of joy in each peculiar mood
Insects of varied taste in rapture share
The heyday luxuries which she comes to heir   40
In wild disorder various routs they run
In water earth still shade and busy sun
And in the crowd of green earths busy claims
They een grow nameless mid their many names
And man that noble insect restless man   45
Whose thoughts scale heaven in its mighty span
Pours forth his living soul in many a shade
And taste runs riot in her every grade
While the low herd mere savages subdued
With nought of feeling or of taste imbued   50
Pass over sweetest scenes a carless eye
As blank as midnight in its deepest dye

From these and different far in rich degrees
Minds spring as various as the leaves of trees
To follow taste and all her sweets explore   55
And Edens make where deserts spread before
In poesys spells some all their raptures find
And revel in the melodies of mind
There nature oer the soul her beauty flings
In all the sweets and essences of things   60
A face of beauty in a city crowd
Met—passed—and vanished like a summer cloud
In poesys vision more refined and fair
Taste reads oerjoyed and greets her image there
Dashes of sunshine and a page of may   65
Live there a whole life long one summers day
A blossom in its witchery of bloom
There gathered dwells in beauty and perfume
The singing bird the brook that laughs along
There ceasless sing and never thirsts for song   70
A pleasing image to its page conferred
In living character and breathing word
Becomes a landscape heard and felt and seen
Sunshine and shade one harmonizing green
Where meads and brooks and forrests basking lie   75
Lasting as truth and the eternal sky
Thus truth to nature as the true sublime
Stands a mount atlas overpeering time
    Styles may with fashions vary—tawdry chaste
Have had their votaries which each fancied taste   80
From Donns old homely gold whose broken feet
Jostles the readers patience from its seat
To Popes smooth rhymes that regularly play
In musics stated periods all the way
That starts and closes starts again and times   85

Its tuning gamut true as minster chimes
From these old fashions stranger metres flow
Half prose half verse that stagger as they go
One line starts smooth and then for room perplext
Elbows along and knocks against the next   90
And half its neighbour where a pause marks time
There the clause ends what follows is for rhyme
Yet truth to nature will in all remain
As grass in winter glorifies the plain
And over fashions foils rise proud and high   95
As lights bright fountain in a cloudy sky
    The man of science in discoverys moods
Roams oer the furze clad heaths leaf buried woods
And by the simple brook in rapture finds
Treasures that wake the laugh of vulgar hinds   100
Who see no further in his dark employs
Then village childern seeking after toys
Their clownish hearts and ever heedless eyes
Find nought in nature they as wealth can prize
With them self interest and the thoughts of gain   105
Are natures beautys all beside are vain
But he the man of science and of taste
Sees wealth far richer in the worthless waste
Where bits of lichen and a sprig of moss
Will all the raptures of his mind engross   110
And bright winged insects on the flowers of may
Shine pearls too wealthy to be cast away
His joys run riot mid each juicy blade
Of grass where insects revel in the shade
And minds of different moods will oft condemn   115
His taste as cruel such the deeds to them
While he unconsious gibbets butterflyes
And strangles beetles all to make us wise

Tastes rainbow visions own unnumbered hues
And every shade its sense of taste pursues   120
The heedless mind may laugh the clown may stare
They own no soul to look for pleasure there
Their grosser feelings in a coarser dress
Mock at the wisdom which they cant possess
Some in recordless rapture love to breath   125
Natures wild Eden wood and field and heath
In common blades of grass his thoughts will raise
A world of beauty to admire and praise
Untill his heart oerflows with swarms of thought
To that great being who raised life from nought   130
The common weed adds graces to his mind
And gleams in beautys few beside may find
Associations sweet each object breeds
And fine ideas upon fancy feeds
He loves not flowers because they shed perfumes   135
Or butterflyes alone for painted plumes
Or birds for singing although sweet it be
But he doth love the wild and meadow lea
There hath the flower its dwelling place and there
The butterflye goes dancing through the air   140
He loves each desolate neglected spot
That seems in labours hurry left forgot
The crank and punished trunk of stunted oak
Freed from its bonds but by the thunder stroke
As crampt by struggling ribs of ivy sere   145
There the glad bird makes home for half the year
But take these several beings from their homes
Each beautious thing a withered thought becomes
Association fades and like a dream
They are but shadows of the things they seem   150
Torn from their homes and happiness they stand

The poor dull captives of a foreign land
Some spruce and delicate ideas feed
With them disorder is an ugly weed
And wood and heath a wilderness of thorns   155
Which gardeners shears nor fashions nor adorns
No spots give pleasure so forlorn and bare
But gravel walks would work rich wonders there
With such wild natures beautys run to waste
And arts strong impulse mars the truth of taste   160
Such are the various moods that taste displays
Surrounding wisdom in concentring rays
Where threads of light from one bright focus run
As days proud halo circles round the sun

                                        March 25th 1825
I TOOK a walk to day to botanize and found that the spring
had taken up her dwelling in good earnest   she has covered
the woods with the white anemonie which the children call
Ladysmocks and the hare bells are just venturing to unfold
their blue dropping bells   the green is covered with daiseys
and the little Celadine   the hedge bottoms are crowded with
the green leaves of the arum were the boy is peeping for
pootys with eager anticipations and delight   the sallows are
cloathed in their golden palms were the bees are singing a
busy welcome to spring   they seem uncommonly fond
of these flowers and gather round them in swarms   I
have often wondered how these little travellers found
their homes agen from the woods and solitudes were
they journey for wax and honey   I have seen them to
day at least 3 miles from any village in Langley wood
working at their palms and some of them with their little
thighs so loaded with the yellow dust as to seem almost

unable to flye   it is curious to see how they collect their load   they keep wiping their legs over their faces to gather the dust that settles there after creeping in the flowers till they have got a sufficient load and then they flye homward to their hives   I have heard that a man curious to know how far his bees travelld in a summers day got up early one morning and stood by one of the hives to powder them as they came out with fine flour to know them agen . . . and having to go to the market that day he passd by a turnip field in full flower about 5 miles from home and to his supprise he found some of his own in their white powderd coats busily huming at their labour with the rest   the Ivy berrys are quite ripe and the wood pigeons are busily fluskering★ among the Ivied dotterels★ on the skirts of the common . . . have you never heard that cronking★ jaring noise in the woods at this early season?   I heard it to day and went into the woods to examine what thing it was that caused the sound and I discoverd that it was the common green woodpecker busily employd at boreing his hole which he effected by twisting his bill round in the way that a carpenter twists his wimble★ with this difference that when he has got it to a certain extent he turns it back and then pecks awhile and then twists agen   his beak seems to serve all the purposes of a nail passer★ gough★ and wimble effectually

First sight of Spring

THE hazel blooms in threads of crimson hue
Peep through the swelling buds and look for spring
Ere yet a white thorn leaf appears in view
Or march finds throstles★ pleased enough to sing

On the old touchwood tree wood peckers cling   5
A moment and their harsh toned notes renew
In happier mood the stockdove claps his wing
The squirrel sputters* up the powdered oak
With tail cocked oer his head and ears errect
Startled to hear the woodmans understroke   10
And with the courage that his fears collect
He hisses fierce half malice and half glee
Leaping from branch to branch about the tree
In winters foliage moss and lichens drest

Wood Pictures in Spring

THE rich brown umber hue the oaks unfold
When springs young sunshine bathes their trunks in gold
So rich so beautiful so past the power
Of words to paint—my heart aches for the dower
The pencil gives to soften and infuse   5
This brown luxuriance of unfolding hues
This living lusious tinting woodlands give
Into a landscape that might breath and live
And this old gate that claps against the tree
The entrance of springs paradise should be   10
Yet paint itself with living nature fails
—The sunshine threading through these broken rails
In mellow shades—no pencil eer conveys
And mind alone feels fancies and pourtrays

May

THE sunshine bathes in clouds of many hues
And mornings feet are gemmed with early dews
Warm Daffodils about the garden beds
Peep thro their pale slim leaves their golden heads
Sweet earthly suns of spring—the gosling broods   5
In coats of sunny green about the road
Waddle in extacy—and in rich moods
The old hen leads her flickering chicks abroad
Oft scuttling neath her wings to see the kite
Hang wavering oer them in the springs blue light   10
The sparrows round their new nests chirp with glee
And sweet the Robin springs young luxury shares
Tuteling its song in feathery gooseberry tree
While watching worms the gardeners spade unbares

Wood pictures in Summer

THE one delicious green that now prevades*
The woods and fields in endless lights and shades
And that deep softness of delicious hues
That overhead blends—softens—and subdues
The eye to extacy and fills the mind   5
With views and visions of enchanting kind
While on the velvet down beneath the swail*
I sit on mossy stulp and broken rail
Or lean oer crippled gate by hugh old tree
Broken by boys disporting there at swee*   10

While sunshine spread from an exaustless sky
Gives all things extacy as well as I
And all wood-swaily places even they
Are joys own tennants keeping holiday

The Wheat ripening

WHAT time the wheat field tinges rusty brown
And barley bleaches in its mellow grey
Tis sweet some smooth mown baulk to wander down
Or cross the fields on footpaths narrow way
Just in the mealy light of waking day   5
As glittering dewdrops moist the maidens gown
And sparkling bounces from her nimble feet
Journeying to milking from the neighbouring town
Making life bright with song—and it is sweet
To mark the grazing herds and list the clown   10
Urge on his ploughing team with cheering calls
And merry shepherds whistling toils begun
And hoarse tongued bird boy whose unceasing calls
Join the larks ditty to the rising sun

Nutters

THE rural occupations of the year
Are each a fitting theme for pastoral song
And pleasing in our autumn paths appear
The groups of nutters as they chat along
The woodland rides in strangest dissabille   5
Maids jacketed grotesque in garments ill

Hiding their elegance of shape—her ways
Her voice of music makes her woman still
Aught else the error of a carless gaze
Might fancy uncouth rustics noising bye   10
With laugh and chat and scraps of morning news
Till met the hazel shades and in they hie
Garbed suiting to the toil—the morning dews
Among the underwood are hardly dry

Yet down with crack and rustle branches come   15
And springing up like bow unloosed when free
Of their ripe clustering bunches brown—while some
Are split and broken under many a tree
Up springs the blundering pheasant with the noise
Loud brawls the maiden to her friends scared sore   20
And loud with mimic voice mischevous boys
Ape stranger voices to affright her more
Eccho long silent answers many a call
Straggling about the wildwoods guessing way
Till by the woodside waiting one and all   25
They gather homward at the close of day
While maids with hastier step from sheperds brawl
Speed on half shamed of their strange dissaray

Emmonsails Heath in winter

I LOVE to see the old heaths withered brake
Mingle its crimpled* leaves with furze and ling
While the old heron from the lonely lake
Starts slow and flaps his melancholly wing

And oddling★ crow in idle motion swing   5
On the half rotten ash trees topmost twig
Beside whose trunk the gipsey makes his bed
Up flies the bouncing woodcock from the brig★
Where a black quagmire quakes beneath the tread
The field fare chatter in the whistling thorn   10
And for the awe★ round fields and closen★ rove
And coy bumbarrels★ twenty in a drove
Flit down the hedge rows in the frozen plain
And hang on little twigs and start again

Winter Fields

O FOR a pleasant book to cheat the sway
Of winter—where rich mirth with hearty laugh
Listens and rubs his legs on corner seat
For fields are mire and sludge—and badly off
Are those who on their pudgy★ paths delay   5
There striding shepherd seeking driest way
Fearing nights wetshod feet and hacking cough
That keeps him waken till the peep of day
Goes shouldering onward and with ready hook
Progs★ oft to ford the sloughs that nearly meet   10
Across the lands—croodling and thin to view
His loath dog follows—stops and quakes and looks
For better roads—till whistled to pursue
Then on with frequent jump he hirkles★ through

Christmass

CHRISTMASS is come and every hearth
Makes room to give him welcome now
Een want will dry its tears in mirth
And crown him wi a holly bough
Tho tramping neath a winters sky   5
Oer snow track paths and ryhmey stiles
The huswife sets her spining bye
And bids him welcome wi her smiles

The shepherd now no more afraid
Since custom doth the chance bestow
Starts up to kiss the giggling maid
Beneath the branch of mizzletoe
That neath each cottage beam is seen   5
Wi pearl-like-berrys shining gay
The shadow still of what hath been
Which fashion yearly fades away

And singers too a merry throng
At early morn wi simple skill   10
Yet imitate the angels song
And chant their christmass ditty still
And mid the storm that dies and swells
By fits—in humings softly steals
The music of the village bells   15
Ringing round their merry peals

And when its past a merry crew
Bedeckt in masks and ribbons gay
The 'Morrice danse' their sports renew
And act their winter evening play   20

The clown-turnd-kings for penny praise
Storm wi the actors strut and swell
And harlequin a laugh to raise
Wears his hump back and tinkling bell

And oft for pence and spicy ale   25
Wi winter nosgays pind before
The wassail singer tells her tale
And drawls her christmass carrols oer
The prentice boy wi ruddy face
And ryhme bepowderd dancing locks   30
From door to door wi happy pace
Runs round to claim his 'christmass box'

AND then the year usd to be crownd with its holidays as
thick as the boughs on a harvest home   there was the long
wishd for Christmass day the celebrated week with two
sundays when we usd to watch the clerk return with his
bundle of ever greens and run for our bunch to stick★ the
windows and empty candlesticks hanging in the corner or
hasten to the woods to gett ivy branches with its joccolate
berrys which our parents usd to color with whitening and the
bluebag sticking the branches behind the pictures on the walls

Winter

OLD January clad in crispy rime
Comes hirpling★ on and often makes a stand
The hasty snowstorm neer disturbs his time
He mends no pace but beats his dithering hand

And February like a timid maid   5
Smiling and sorrowing follows in his train
Huddled in cloak of mirey roads affraid
She hastens on to greet her home again
Then March the prophetess by storms inspired
Gazes in rapture on the troubled sky   10
And then in headlong fury madly fired
She bids the hail storm boil and hurry bye
Yet neath the blackest cloud a sunbeam flings
Its cheering promise of returning spring

Wood pictures in winter

THE woodland swamps with mosses varified
And bullrush forrests bowing by the side
Of shagroot sallows that snug shelter make
For the coy morehen in her bushy lake
Into whose tide a little runnel weaves   5
Such charms for silence through the choaking leaves
A whimpling* melodys that but intrude
As lullabys to ancient solitude
The wood grass plats which last year left behind
Weaving their feathery lightness to the wind   10
Look now as picturesque amid the scene
As when the summer glossed their stems in green
While hasty hare brunts* through the creepy gap
Seeks the soft beds and squats in safetys lap

BLACKBIRDS and Thrushes particularly the former feed in
hard winters upon the shell snail horns by hunting them from

the hedge bottoms and wood stulps and taking them to a
stone where they brake them in a very dexterous manner   any curious observer of nature may see in hard frosts
the shells of pootys thickly litterd round a stone in the lanes
and if he waits a short time he will quickly see one of these
birds coming with a snailhorn in his bill which he constantly
taps on the stone till it is broken   he then extracts the snail
and like a true sportsman eagerly hastens to hunt them again
in the hedges or woods where a frequent rustle of their little
feet is heard among the dead leaves

Signs of Winter

Tis winter plain the images around
Protentious★ tell us of the closing year
Short grows the stupid day the moping fowl
Go roost at noon—upon the mossy barn
The thatcher hangs and lays the frequent yaum   5
Nudged close to stop the rain that drizzling falls
With scarce one interval of sunny sky
For weeks still leeking on that sulky gloom
Muggy and close a doubt twixt night and day
The sparrow rarely chirps the thresher pale   10
Twanks★ with sharp measured raps the weary frail★
Thump after thump right tiresome to the ear
The hedger lonesome brustles at his toil
And shepherds trudge the fields without a song

The cat runs races with her tail—the dog   15
Leaps oer the orchard hedge and knarls⋆ the grass
The swine run round and grunt and play with straw
Snatching out hasty mouthfuls from the stack
Sudden upon the elm tree tops the crows
Unceremonious visit pays and croaks   20
Then swops⋆ away—from mossy barn the owl
Bobs hasty out—wheels round and scared as soon
As hastily retires—the ducks grow wild
And from the muddy pond fly up and wheel
A circle round the village and soon tired   25
Plunge in the pond again—the maids in haste
Snatch from the orchard hedge the mizled⋆ cloaths
And laughing hurry in to keep them dry

The Flood

ON LOLHAM BRIGS in wild and lonely mood
Ive seen the winter floods their gambols play
Through each old arch that trembled while I stood
Bent oer its wall to watch the dashing spray
As their old stations would be washed away   5
Crash came the ice against the jambs and then
A shudder jarred the arches—yet once more
It breasted raving waves and stood agen
To wait the shock as stubborn as before
—White foam brown crested with the russet soil   10
As washed from new ploughd lands would dart beneath
Then round and round a thousand eddies boil

On tother side—then pause as if for breath
One minute—and ingulphed—like life in death

Whose wrecky stains dart on the floods away   15
More swift then shadows in a stormy day
Straws trail and turn and steady—all in vain
The engulphing arches shoot them quickly through
The feather dances flutters and again
Darts through the deepest dangers still afloat   20
Seeming as faireys whisked it from the view
And danced it oer the waves as pleasures boat
Light hearted as a merry thought in may—
Trays—uptorn bushes—fence demolished rails
Loaded with weeds in sluggish motions stray   25
Like water monsters lost each winds and trails
Till near the arches—then as in affright
It plunges—reels—and shudders out of sight

Waves trough—rebound—and fury boil again
Like plunging monsters rising underneath   30
Who at the top curl up a shaggy main
A moment catching at a surer breath
Then plunging headlong down and down—and on
Each following boil the shadow of the last
And other monsters rise when those are gone   35
Crest their fringed waves—plunge onward and are past
—The chill air comes around me ocean blea
From bank to bank the waterstrife is spread
Strange birds like snow spots oer the huzzing* sea
Hang where the wild duck hurried past and fled   40
On roars the flood—all restless to be free
Like trouble wandering to eternity

Summer Images

Now swathy summer by rude health embrowned
Presedence takes of rosey fingered spring
And laughing joy with wild flowers prankt★ and crowned
   A wild and giddy thing
With health robust from every care unbound   5
   Comes on the zephers wing
   And cheers the toiling clown

Happy as holiday enjoying face
Loud tongued and 'merry as a marriage bell'
Thy lightsome step sheds joy in every place   10
   And where the troubled dwell
Thy witching smiles weans them of half their cares
   And from thy sunny spell
   They greet joy unawares

Then with thy sultry locks all loose and rude   15
And mantle laced with gems of garish light
Come as of wont—for I would fain intrude
   And in the worlds despite
Share the rude mirth that thine own heart beguiles
   If haply so I might   20
   Win pleasure from thy smiles

Me not the noise of brawling pleasures cheer
In nightly revels or in city streets
But joys which sooth and not distract mine ear
   That one at leisure meets   25
In the green woods and meadows summer shorn
   Or fields where bee flye greets
   Ones ear with mellow horn

Where green swathed grass hopper on treble pipe
Singeth and danceth in mad hearted pranks   30
And bees go courting every flower thats ripe
    On baulks★ and sunny banks
And droning dragon flye on rude bassoon
    Striveth to give God thanks
    In no discordant tune   35

Where speckled thrush by self delight embued
Singeth unto himself for joys amends
And drinks the honey dew of solitude
    Where happiness attends
With inbred joy untill his heart oerflows   40
    Of which the worlds rude friends
    Nought heeding nothing knows

Where the gay river laughing as it goes
Plashes with easy wave its flaggy sides
And to the calm of heart in calmness shows   45
    What pleasure there abides
To trace its sedgy banks from trouble free
    Spots solitude provides
    To muse and happy be

Or ruminating neath some pleasant bush   50
On sweet silk grasses stretch me at mine ease
Where I can pillow on the yielding rush
    And acting as I please
Drop into pleasant dreams or musing lye
    Mark the wind shaken trees   55
    And cloud betravelled sky

And think me how some barter joy for care
And waste lifes summer health in riot rude
Of nature nor of natures sweets aware
   Where passions vain intrude   60
These by calm musings softened are and still
   And the hearts better mood
   Feels sick of doing ill

Here I can live and at my leisure seek
Joys far from cold restraints—not fearing pride   65
Free as the winds that breath upon my cheek
   Rude health so long denied
Where poor integrity can sit at ease
   And list self satisfied
   The song of honey bees   70

And green lane traverse heedless where it goes
Naught guessing till some sudden turn espies
Rude battered finger post that stooping shows
   Where the snug mystery lies
And then a mossy spire with ivy crown   75
   Clears up the short supprise
   And shows the peeping town

And see the wild flowers in their summer morn
Of beauty feeding on joys luscious hours
The gay convolvulus wreathing round the thorn   80
   Agape for honey showers
And slender king cup burnished with the dew
   Of mornings early hours
   Like gold yminted new

And mark by rustic bridge oer shallow stream   85
Cow tending boy to toil unreconsiled
Absorbed as in some vagrant summer dream
   And now in gestures wild
Starts dancing to his shadow on the wall
   Feeling self gratified   90
   Nor fearing human thrall

Then thread the sunny valley laced with streams
Or forrests rude and the oershadowed brims
Of simple ponds where idle shepherd dreams
   And streaks* his listless limbs   95
Or trace* hay scented meadow smooth and long
   Where joys wild impulse swims
   In one continued song

I love at early morn from new mown swath*
To see the startled frog his rout* pursue   100
And mark while leaping oer the dripping path
   His bright sides scatter dew
And early lark that from its bustle flyes—
   To hail his mattin new
   And watch him to the skyes   105

And note on hedgerow baulks in moisture sprent*
The jetty snail creep from the mossy thorn
In earnest heed and tremolous intent
   Frail brother of the morn
That from the tiney bents* and misted leaves   110
   Withdraws his timid horn
   And fearful vision weaves

And swallows heed on smoke tanned chimney top
As wont be first unsealing mornings eye
Ere yet the bee hath gleaned one wayward drop   115
   Of honey on his thigh
And see him seek morns airy couch to sing
   Untill the golden sky
   Besprents his russet wing

And sawning★ boy by tanning corn espy   120
With clapping noise to startle birds away
And hear him bawl to every passer bye
   To know the hour of day
And see the uncradled breeze refreshed and strong
   With waking blossoms play   125
   And breath eolian song

I love the south west wind or low or loud
And not the less when sudden drops of rain
Moistens my glowing cheek from ebon cloud
   Threatening soft showers again   130
That over lands new ploughed and meadow grounds
   Summers sweet breath unchains
   And wakes harmonious sounds

Rich music breaths in summers every sound
And in her harmony of varied greens   135
Woods meadows hedgrows cornfields all around
   Much beauty intervenes
Filling with harmony the ear and eye
   While oer the mingling scenes
   Far spreads the laughing sky   140

And wind enarmourd aspin—mark the leaves
Turn up their silver lining to the sun
And list the brustling noise that oft decieves
   And make the sheep boy run
The sound so mimics fast approaching showers   145
   He thinks the rain begun
   And hastes to sheltering bowers

And mark the evening curdle dank and grey
Changing her watchet* hue for sombre weed
And moping owl to close the lids of day   150
   On drowsy wing proceed
While chickering* cricket tremolous and long
   Lights farewell inly heeds
   And gives it parting song

While pranking* bat its flighty circlet makes   155
And gloworm burnisheth its lamp anew
Oer meadows dew besprent—and beetle wakes
   Enquiries ever new
Teazing each passing ear with murmurs vain
   As wonting to pursue   160
   His homeward path again

And catch the melody of distant bells
That on the wind with pleasing hum rebounds
By fitful starts—then musically swells
   Oer the dim stilly grounds   165
While on the meadow bridge the pausing boy
   Listens the mellow sounds
   And hums in vacant joy

And now the homebound hedger bundles round
His evening faggot and with every stride   170
His leathern doublet leaves a rusling sound
   Till silly sheep beside
His path start tremolous and once again
   Look back dissatisfied
   And scan the dewy plain   175

And greet the soothing calm that smoothly stills
Oer the hearts every sense its opiate dews
In meek eyed moods and ever balmy trills
   That softens and subdues
With gentle quiets bland and sober train   180
   Which dreamy eve renews
   In many a mellow strain

I love to walk the fields they are to me
A legacy no evil can destroy
They like a spell set every rapture free   185
   That cheered me when a boy
Play pastime—all times blotting pen conseals
   Come like a new born joy
   To greet me in the fields

For natures objects ever harmonize   190
With emulous taste that vulgar deed anoys
It loves in quiet moods to sympathise
   And meet vibrating joys
Oer natures pleasant things—nor slighting deems
   Pastimes the muse employs   195
   As vain obtrusive themes

Summer Moods

I LOVE at eventide to walk alone
Down narrow lanes oerhung with dewy thorn
Where from the long grass underneath the snail
Jet black creeps out and sprouts his timid horn
I love to muse oer meadows newly mown   5
Where withering grass perfumes the sultry air
Where bees search round with sad and weary drone
In vain for flowers that bloomed but newly there
While in the juicey corn the hidden quail
Cries 'wet my foot' and hid as thoughts unborn   10
The fairy like and seldom-seen land rail
Utters 'craik craik' like voices underground
Right glad to meet the evenings dewy veil
And see the light fade into glooms around

A Autumn Morning

THE autumn morning waked by many a gun
Throws oer the fields her many coloured light
Wood wildly touched close tanned and stubbles dun
A motley paradise for earths delight
Clouds ripple as the darkness breaks to light   5
And clover fields are hid with silver mist
One shower of cobwebs oer the surface spread
And threads of silk in strange disorder twist
Round every leaf and blossoms bottly head
Hares in the drowning herbage scarcely steal   10

But on the battered pathway squats abed
And by the cart rut nips her morning meal
Look where we may the scene is strange and new
And every object wears a changing hue

THOUGHT I was up sooner then usual and before morning
was on the stir out of doors   but I am pleasantly disapointed
by the whistle of the ploughboy past the window making
himself merry and trying to make the dull weather dance to a
very pleasant tune which I know well and yet cannot recollect
the song   but there are hundreds of these pleasant tunes
familiar to the plough and the splashing team and the little
fields of spring that have lain out the brown rest of winter and
green into mirth with the sprouting grain the songs of the
sky lark and the old songs and ballads that ever accompany
field happiness in following the plough—but neither heard
known or noticed by all the world beside

Early Images

COME early morning with thy mealy grey
Moist grass and fitful gales that winnow soft
And frequent—Ill be up with early day
And roam the social way where passing oft
The milking maid who greets the pleasant morn   5
And shepherd with his hook in folded arm
Rocking along accross the bending corn
And hear the many sounds from distant farm
Of cackling hens and turkeys gobbling loud
And teams just plodding on their way to plough   10

Down russet tracks that strip the closen green
And hear the mellow low of distant cow
And see the mist up creeping like a cloud
From hollow places in the early scene

And mark the jerking swallow jerk and fling   15
Its flight oer new mown meadows happily
And cuckoo quivering upon narrow wing
Take sudden flitting from the neighbouring tree
And heron stalking solitary thing
Mount up into high travel far away   20
And that mild indecision hanging round
Skys holding bland communion with the ground
In gentlest pictures of the infant day
Now picturing rain—while many a pleasing sound
Grows mellower distant in the mealy grey   25
Of dewy pastures and full many a sight
Seems sweeter in its indistinct array
Than when it glows in mornings stronger light

The morning wind

THERES more then music in this early wind
Awaking like a bird refreshed from sleep
And joy what Adam might in eden find
When he with angels did communion keep
It breaths all balm and insence from the sky   5
Blessing the husbandman with freshening powers
Joys manna from its wings doth fall and lie
Harvests for early wakers with the flowers

The very grass in joys devotion moves
Cowslaps in adoration and delight   10
This way and that bow to the breath they love
Of the young winds that with the dew pearls play
Till smoking chimneys sicken the young light
And feelings fairey visions fade away

Winter Evening

THE crib stock fothered*—horses suppered up
And cows in sheds all littered down in straw
The threshers gone the owls are left to whoop
The ducks go waddling with distended craw
Through little hole made in the henroost door   5
And geese with idle gabble never oer
Bate* careless hog untill he tumbles down
Insult provoking spite to noise the more
While fowl high perched blink with contemptuous frown
On all the noise and bother heard below   10
Over the stable ridge in crowds the crow
With jackdaws intermixed known by their noise
To the warm woods behind the village go
And whistling home for bed go weary boys

Evening school boys

HARKEN that happy shout—the school house door
Is open thrown and out the younkers* teem
Some run to leap frog on the rushy moor
And others dabble in the shallow stream

Catching young fish and turning pebbles oer   5
For muscle* clams—Look in that mellow gleam
Where the retiring sun that rests the while
Streams through the broken hedge—How happy seem
Those schoolboy friendships leaning oer the stile
Both reading in one book—anon a dream   10
Rich with new joys doth their young hearts beguile
And the books pocketed most hastily
Ah happy boys well may ye turn and smile
When joys are yours that never cost a sigh

Mist in the Meadows

THE evening oer the meadow seems to stoop
More distant lessens the diminished spire
Mist in the hollows reaks and curdles up
Like fallen clouds that spread—and things retire
Less seen and less—the shepherd passes near   5
And little distant most grotesquely shades
As walking without legs—lost to his knees
As through the rawky* creeping smoke he wades
Now half way up the arches dissappear
And small the bits of sky that glimmer through   10
Then trees loose all but tops—while fields remain
As wont—the indistinctness passes bye
The shepherd all his length is seen again
And further on the village meets the eye

Happiness of evening

THE winter wind with strange and fearful gust
Stirs the dark wood and in the lengthy night
Howls in the chimney top while fears mistrust
Listens the noise by the small glimmering light
Of cottage hearth where warm a circle sits   5
Of happy dwellers telling morts of tales
Where some long memory wakens up by fits
Laughter and fear and over all prevails
Wonder predominant—they sit and hear
The very hours to minutes and the song   10
Or story be the subject what it may
Is ever found too short and never long
While the uprising tempest loudly roars
And boldest hearts fear stirring out of doors

Fears ignorance their fancy only harms   15
Doors safely locked fear only entrance wins
While round the fire in every corner warms
Till nearest hitch away and rub their shins
And now the tempest in its plight begins
The shutters jar the woodbine on the wall   20
Rustles agen the panes and over all
The noisey storm to troublous fancy dins
And pity stirs the stoutest heart to call
'Who's there' as slow the door latch seemly stirred
But nothing answered so the sounds they heard   25
Was no benighted traveller—and they fall
To telling pleasant tales to conquor fear
And sing a merry song till bed time creepeth near

Cottage Fears

THE evening gathers from the gloomy woods
And darkling creeps oer silent vale and hill
While the snug village in nights happy moods
Is resting calm and beautifully still
The windows gleam with light the yelping curs   5
That guards the henroost from the thieving fox
Barks now and then as somthing passing stirs
And distant dogs the noises often mocks
While foxes from the woods send dismal cries
Like somthing in distress the cottager   10
Hears the dread noise and thinks of danger nigh
And locks up door in haste—nor cares to stir
From the snug safety of his humble shed
Then tells strange tales till time to go to bed

'WILL with a whisp' 'Jinny Whisk' 'Jack with a Lanthorn'
—in this november month they are often out in the dark
misty nights—on Rotten Moor Dead Moor Eastwell moor
Banton Green end Lolham Briggs Rinedyke furlong and
many other places in the lordship   I have myself seen them
on most of these spots   one dark night I was coming accross
the new parks when a sudden light wild and pale appea[r]ed
all round me on my left hand for a hundred yards or more
accompanied by a crackling noise like that of peas straw
burning   I stood looking for a minute or so and felt rather
alarmed when darkness came round me again and one of the
dancing jack a la[n]thorns was whisking away in the distance

over the Nunton bridge a light like a lanthorn standing on the
wall of the other bridge   I kept my eyes on it for a while and
hastened to come up to it but ere I got half over the meadow
it suddenly fell and tumbled into the stream   and when I got
on the bridge I looked down it and saw the will o whi[s]p
vapour like a light in a bladder whisking along close to the
water as if swimming along its surface   but what supprised
me was that it was going contrary to the stream

Night Wind

DARKNESS like midnight from the sobbing woods
Clamours with dismal tidings of the rain
Roaring as rivers breaking loose in floods
To spread and foam and deluge all the plain
The cotter★ listens at his door again   5
Half doubting wether it be floods or wind
And through the thickening darkness looks affraid
Thinking of roads that travel has to find
Through nights black depths in dangers garb arrayed
And the loud glabber★ round the flaze★ soon stops   10
When hushed to silence by the lifted hand
Of fearing dame who hears the noise in dread
And thinks a deluge comes to drown the land
Nor dares she go to bed untill the tempest drops

Sabbath Bells

IVE often on a sabbath day
Where pastoral quiet dwells
Lay down among the new mown hay
To listen distant bells

That beautifully flung the sound   5
Upon the quiet wind
While beans in blossom breathed around
A fragrance oer the mind

A fragrance and a joy beside
That never wears away   10
The very air seems deified
Upon a sabbath day
So beautiful the flitting wrack
Slow pausing from the eye
Earths music seemed to call them back   15
Calm settled in the sky

And I have listened till I felt
A feeling not in words
A love that rudest moods would melt
When those sweet sounds was heard   20
A melancholly joy at rest
A pleasurable pain
A love a rapture of the breast
That nothing will explain

A dream of beauty that displays   25
Imaginary joys
That all the world in all its ways
Finds not to realize
All idly stretched upon the hay
The wind flirt fanning bye   30
How soft how sweetly swept away
The music of the sky

The ear it lost and caught the sound
Swelled beautifully on
A fitful melody around   35
Of sweetness heard and gone
I felt such thoughts I yearned to sing
The humming airs delight
That seemed to move the swallows wing
Into a wilder flight   40

The butterflye in wings of brown
Would find me where I lay
Fluttering and bobbing up and down
And settling on the hay
The waving blossoms seemed to throw   45
Their fragrance to the sound
While up and down and loud and low
The bells were ringing round

Beans in Blossom

THE south west wind how pleasant in the face
It breathes while sauntering in a musing pace
I roam these new ploughed fields and by the side
Of this old wood where happy birds abide
And the rich blackbird through his golden bill   5
Litters wild music when the rest are still
Now luscious comes the scent of blossomed beans
That oer the path in rich disorder leans
Mid which the bees in busy songs and toils
Load home luxuriantly their yellow spoils   10

The herd cows toss the molehills in their play
And often stand the strangers steps at bay
Mid clover blossoms red and tawney white
Strong scented with the summers warm delight

Stray Walks

How pleasant are the fields to roam and think
Whole sabbaths through unnoticed and alone
Beside the little mole hill skirted brink
Of the small brook that skips oer many a stone
Or green woodside where many a squatting oak   5
Far oer grass screeds their white stained branches hing★
Forming in pleasant close a happy seat
To nestle in while small birds chirp and sing
And the loud blackbird will its mate provoke
More louder yet its chorus to repeat   10
How pleasant is it thus to think and roam
The many paths scarce knowing which to chuse
All full of pleasant scenes—then wander home
And oer the beautys we have met to muse

Tis sunday and the little paths that wind   15
Through closen green by hedges and wood sides
And like a brook corn crowded slope divides
Of pleasant fields—their frequent passers find
From early morn to mellow close of day
On different errands climbing many stiles   20
Oer hung with awthorn tempting haste to stay
And cool some moments of the road away

When hot and high the uncheckt summer smiles
Some journeying to the little hamlet hid
In dark surrounding trees to see their friends   25
While some sweet leisures aimless road pursue
Wherever fancys musing pleasure wends
To woods or lakes or church thats never out of view

Wood Rides

WHO hath not felt the influence that so calms
The weary mind in summers sultry hours
When wandering thickest woods beneath the arms
Of ancient oaks and brushing nameless flowers
That verge the little ride who hath not made   5
A minutes waste of time and sat him down
Upon a pleasant swell to gaze awhile
On crowding ferns bluebells and hazel leaves
And showers of lady smocks so called by toil
When boys sprote* gathering sit on stulps and weave   10
Garlands while barkmen pill the fallen tree
—Then mid the green variety to start
Who hath [not] met that mood from turmoil free
And felt a placid joy refreshed at heart

The Ragwort

RAGWORT thou humble flower with tattered leaves
I love to see thee come and litter gold
What time the summer binds her russet sheaves
Decking rude spots in beautys marigold
That without thee were dreary to behold   5

Sun burnt and bare—the meadow bank the baulk
That leads a waggonway through mellow fields
Rich with the tints that harvests plenty yields
Browms of all hues—and every where I walk
Thy waste of shining blossoms richly shields   10
The sun tanned sward in splendid hues that burn
So bright and glaring that the very light
Of the rich sunshine doth to paleness turn
And seems but very shadows in thy sight

I ALWAYS admire the kindling freshness that the bark of the
different sorts of trees and underwood asume in the forest—
the 'foul royce' twigs kindling into a vivid color at their tops
as red as woodpiegons claws the ash with its grey bark and
black swelling buds the Birch with its 'paper rind' and the
darker mottled sorts of hazle black alder with the greener
hues of sallows willows and the bramble that still wears its
leaves with the privet of a purple hue while the straggling
wood briar shines in a brighter and more beautiful green   odd
forward branches in the new laid hedges of white thorn begin
to freshen into green before the arum dare peep out of its
hood or the primrose and violet shoot up a new leaf thro the
warm moss and ivy that shelter their spring dwellings   the
furze too on the common wear a fairer green and here and
there an odd branch is coverd with golden flowers and the
ling or heath nestling among the long grass below (coverd
with the witherd flowers of last year) is sprouting up into
fresh hopes of spring   the fairey rings on the pasture are
getting deeper dyes and the water weeds with long silver
green blades of grass are mantling the stagnant ponds in their
summer liverys
                    [dated Feb 7, 1825]

The Hollow Tree

How oft a summer shower hath started me
To seek for shelter in a hollow tree
Old hugh ash dotterel wasted to a shell
Whose vigorous head still grew and flourished well
Where ten might sit upon the battered floor   5
And still look round discovering room for more
And he who chose a hermit life to share
Might have a door and make a cabin there
They seemed so like a house that our desires
Would call them so and make our gipsey fires   10
And eat field dinners of the juicey peas
Till we were wet and drabbled* to the knees
But in our old tree house rain as it might
Not one drop fell although it rained till night

Salters Tree

Hugh Elm thy rifted trunk all notched and scarred
Like to a warriors destiny—I love
To stretch me often on such shadowed sward
And hear the sighs of summer leaves above
Or on thy buttressed roots to sit and lean   5
In carless attitude and there reflect
On times and deeds and darings that have been
Old cast aways now swallowed in neglect
While thou art towering in thy strength of heart
Stirring the soul to vain imaginings   10
In which lifes sordid being hath no part
The wind in that eternal ditty sings
Humming of future things that burns the mind
To leave some fragment of itself behind

The Crab Tree

SPRING comes anew and brings each little pledge
That still as wont my childish heart decieves
I stoop again for violets in the hedge
Among the ivy and old withered leaves
And often mark amid the clumps of sedge   5
The pooty shells I gathered when a boy
But cares have claimed me many an evil day
And chilled the relish which I had for joy
Yet when crab blossoms blush among the may
As wont in years gone bye I scramble now   10
Up mid the bramble for my old esteems
Filling my hands with many a blooming bough
Till the heart stirring past as present seems
Save the bright sunshine of those fairy dreams

AND be it further Enacted, That no Horses, Beasts, Asses,
Sheep, Lambs, or other Cattle, shall at any Time within
the first Ten Years after the said Allotments shall be directed
to be entered upon by the respective Proprietors thereof, be
kept in any of the public Carriage Roads or Ways to be set
out and fenced off on both Sides, or Laned out in pursuance of
this Act.

[From: An Act for Inclosing Lands in the Parishes of Maxey
     ... and Helpstone, in the County of Northampton,
     49 Geo. III. *Sess.* 1809.]

The Mores

FAR spread the moorey ground a level scene
Bespread with rush and one eternal green
That never felt the rage of blundering plough
Though centurys wreathed springs blossoms on its brow
Still meeting plains that stretched them far away   5
In uncheckt shadows of green brown and grey
Unbounded freedom ruled the wandering scene
Nor fence of ownership crept in between
To hide the prospect of the following eye
Its only bondage was the circling sky   10
One mighty flat undwarfed by bush and tree
Spread its faint shadow of immensity
And lost itself which seemed to eke its bounds
In the blue mist the orisons edge surrounds

Now this sweet vision of my boyish hours   15
Free as spring clouds and wild as summer flowers
Is faded all—a hope that blossomed free
And hath been once no more shall ever be
Inclosure came and trampled on the grave
Of labours rights and left the poor a slave   20
And memorys pride ere want to wealth did bow
Is both the shadow and the substance now
The sheep and cows were free to range as then
Where change might prompt nor felt the bonds of men
Cows went and came with evening morn and night   25
To the wild pasture as their common right
And sheep unfolded with the rising sun
Heard the swains shout and felt their freedom won
Tracked the red fallow field and heath and plain
Then met the brook and drank and roamed again   30

The brook that dribbled on as clear as glass
Beneath the roots they hid among the grass
While the glad shepherd traced their tracks along
Free as the lark and happy as her song
But now alls fled and flats of many a dye   35
That seemed to lengthen with the following eye
Moors loosing from the sight far smooth and blea
Where swopt the plover in its pleasure free
Are vanished now with commons wild and gay
As poets visions of lifes early day   40
Mulberry bushes where the boy would run
To fill his hands with fruit are grubbed★ and done
And hedgrow briars—flower lovers overjoyed
Came and got flower pots—these are all destroyed
And sky bound mores in mangled garbs are left   45
Like mighty giants of their limbs bereft
Fence now meets fence in owners little bounds
Of field and meadow large as garden grounds
In little parcels little minds to please
With men and flocks imprisoned ill at ease   50
Each little path that led its pleasant way
As sweet as morning leading night astray
Where little flowers bloomed round a varied host
That travel felt delighted to be lost
Nor grudged the steps that he had taen as vain   55
When right roads traced his journeys and again
Nay on a broken tree hed sit awhile
To see the mores and fields and meadows smile
Sometimes with cowslaps smothered—then all white
With daiseys—then the summers splendid sight   60
Of corn fields crimson oer the 'headach' bloomd
Like splendid armys for the battle plumed
He gazed upon them with wild fancys eye

As fallen landscapes from an evening sky
These paths are stopt—the rude philistines thrall   65
Is laid upon them and destroyed them all
Each little tyrant with his little sign
Shows where man claims earth glows no more divine
But paths to freedom and to childhood dear
A board sticks up to notice 'no road here'   70
And on the tree with ivy overhung
The hated sign by vulgar taste is hung
As tho the very birds should learn to know
When they go there they must no further go
This with the poor scared freedom bade good bye   75
And much they feel it in the smothered sigh
And birds and trees and flowers without a name
All sighed when lawless laws enclosure came
And dreams of plunder in such rebel schemes
Have found too truly that they were but dreams   80

Apology for the Poor

Mr Editor

In this suprising stir of patrioutism and wonderful change in
the ways and opinions of men when your paper is weekly
loaded with the free speech[e]s of county meetings can you
find room for mine? or will you hear the voice of a poor
man?—I only wish to ask you a few plain questions

Amidst all this stir about taxation and tythes and agricultural distress are the poor to recieve corresponding
benefits   they have been told so I know but it is not the first
time they have heard that and been dissapointed   when the
tax was taken from leather they was told they should have

shoes almost for nothing and they heard the parliment speeches
of patriots as the forthcoming propechys of a political
millenium but their hopes were soon frost bitten for the
tax has long vanished and the price of shoes remains just were
it did   nay I believe they are a trifle dearer then they was
then—thats the only difference   then there was a hue and
cry about taking off the duty of Sp[i]ritous liquors and the
best Gin was to be little more in price then small beer   the
poor man shook his head over such speeches and looking at
his shoes had no faith to believe any more of these cheap
wonders so he was not dissapointed in finding gin as dear as
ever—for which he had little to regret for he prefered good
ale to any spirits   and now the Malt and beer tax is in full
cry what is the poor man to expect   it may benefit the farmers
a little and the common brewers a good deal and there no
doubt the matter will end   the poor man will not find the
refuse of any more use to him then a dry bone to a hungry
dog—excuse the simile reader for the poor have been likened
unto dogs before now   and many other of these time serving
hue and cries might be noticed in which the poor man was
promised as much benefit as the stork was in the fable for
pulling out the bone from the Wolfs throat and who got
just as much at last as the stork did for his pains

some of the patriots of these meetings seem to consider the
corn law as a bone sticking in the throat of the countrys
distress but I am sure that the poor man will be no better off
in such a matter—he will only be 'burning his fingers' and not
filling his belly by harbouring any notions of benefit from
that quarter for he is so many degrees lower in the Thremo-
meter of distress that such benefits to others will not reach
him and tho the Farmers should again be in their summer
splendour of 'high prices' and 'better markets' as they phrase
it the poor man would still be found very little above freezing

point—at least I very much fear so for I speak from experience
and not from hearsay and hopes as some do   some years
back when grain sold at 5 and 6 guineas a quarter I can point
out a many villages where the Farmers under a combination
for each others inter[e]sts would give no more in winter then
10 shillings per Week   I will not say that all did so for in a
many places and at that very time Farmers whose good
intentions was 'to live and let live' gave from 12 to 15 shillings
per week and these men would again do the same thing but
they could not compel others and there it is were the poor
man looses the benefit that ought to fall to him from the
farmers 'better markets' and 'high prices' for corn   I hope
Mr Editor that I do not offend by my plain speaking for I
wish only to be satisfied about these few particulars and I
am so little of a politician that I would rather keep out of the
crowd then that my hobnails should trample on the gouty
toes of any one   tho I cannot help thinking when I read your
paper that there is a vast number of taxable advocates wearing
barrack shoes or they would certainly not leave the advocates
for reform to acchieve their triumphs without a struggle   I
wish the good of the people may be found at the end and that
in the general triumph the poor man may not be forgotten   for the poor have many oppressors and no voice to be
heard above them   he is a dumb burthen in the scorn of the
worlds prosperity yet in its adversity they are found ever
ready to aid and assist and tho that be but as the widows mite
yet his honest feelings in the cause are as worthy as the orators
proudest orations   Being a poor man myself I am naturally
wishing to see some one become the advocate and champion
for the poor not in his speeches but his actions   for speeches
are now adays nothing but words and sound   Politicians are
known to be exceedingly wise as far as regards themselves
and we have heard of one who tho his whole thoughts

seemd constantly professing the good of his country yet he
was cunning enough to keep one thought to himself in the
hour of danger when he luckily hit upon the thought of
standing upon his hat to keep himself from catching cold
not to die for the good of the country as some others did and
to be alive as he is at this moment   now if the poor mans
chance at these meetings is any thing better then being a sort
of foot cushion for the benefit of others I shall be exceedingly
happy but as it is I much fear it as the poor mans lot seems to
have been so long remembered as to be entirely forgotten

I am sir your humble Servant
A Poor Man

Remembrances

SUMMERS pleasures they are gone like to visions every one
And the cloudy days of autumn and of winter cometh on
I tried to call them back but unbidden they are gone
Far away from heart and eye and for ever far away
Dear heart and can it be that such raptures meet decay   5
I thought them all eternal when by Langley bush I lay
I thought them joys eternal when I used to shout and play
On its banks at clink and bandy chock★ and taw and
   ducking stone★
Where silence sitteth now on the wild heath as her own
Like a ruin of the past all alone   10

When I used to lye and sing by old eastwells boiling spring
When I used to tie the willow boughs together for a swing
And fish with crooked pins and thread and never catch a
   thing
With heart just like a feather—now as heavy as a stone

When beneath old lea close oak I the bottom branches
   broke   15
To make out harvest cart like so many working folk
And then to cut a straw at the brook to have a soak
O I never dreamed of parting or that trouble had a sting
Or that pleasures like a flock of birds would ever take to
   wing
Leaving nothing but a little naked spring   20

When jumping time away on old cross berry way
And eating awes★ like sugar plumbs ere they had lost the
   may
And skipping like a leveret before the peep of day
On the rolly poly up and down of pleasant Swordy well
When in round oaks narrow lane as the south got black
   again   25
We sought the hollow ash that was shelter from the rain
With our pockets full of pease we had stolen from the grain
How delicious was the dinner time on such a showery day
O words are poor reciepts★ for what time hath stole away
The ancient pulpit trees and the play   30

When for school oer little field with its brook and wooden
   brig
Where I swaggered like a man though I was not half so big
While I held my little plough though twas but a willow
   twig
And drove my team along made of nothing but a name
'Gee hep' and 'hoit' and 'woi'—O I never call to mind   35
Those pleasant names of places but I leave a sigh behind
While I see the little mouldiwarps★ hang sweeing to the
   wind
On the only aged willow that in all the field remains

And nature hides her face while theyre sweeing in their
    chains
And in a silent murmuring complains   40

Here was commons for their hills where they seek for free-
    dom still
Though every commons gone and though traps are set to
    kill
The little homeless miners—O it turns my bosom chill
When I think of old 'sneap green' puddocks nook and hilly
    snow
Where bramble bushes grew and the daisey gemmed in
    dew   45
And the hills of silken grass like to cushions on the view
Where we threw the pismire* crumbs when we'd nothing
    else to do
All leveled like a desert by the never weary plough
All banished like the sun where that cloud is passing now
And settled here for ever on its brow   50

O I never thought that joys would run away from boys
Or that boys should change their minds and forsake mid-
    summer joys
But alack I never dreamed that the world had other toys
To petrify first feelings like the fable into stone
Till I found the pleasure past and a winter come at last   55
Then the fields were sudden bare and the sky got over cast
And boy hoods pleasing haunts like a blossom in the blast
Was shrivelled to a withered weed and trampled down and
    done
Till vanished was the morning spring and set the summer
    sun
And winter fought her battle strife and won   60

By Langley bush I roam but the bush hath lefts its hill
On cowper green I stray tis a desert strange and chill
And spreading lea close oak ere decay had penned its will
To the axe of the spoiler and self interest fell a prey
And crossberry way and old round oaks narrow lane   65
With its hollow trees like pulpits I shall never see again
Inclosure like a buonaparte let not a thing remain
It levelled every bush and tree and levelled every hill
And hung the moles for traitors—though the brook is
    running still
It runs a naked stream cold and chill   70

O had I known as then joy had left the paths of men
I had watched her night and day besure and never slept agen
And when she turned to go O I'd caught her mantle then
And wooed her like a lover by my lonely side to stay
Aye knelt and worshiped on as love in beautys bower   75
And clung upon her smiles as a bee upon a flower
And gave her heart my poesys all cropt in a sunny hour
As keepsakes and pledges all to never fade away
But love never heeded to treasure up the may
So it went the common road to decay   80

The Flitting

IVE left my own old home of homes
Green fields and every pleasant place
The summer like a stranger comes
I pause and hardly know her face
I miss the hazels happy green   5
The blue bells quiet hanging blooms
Where envy's sneer was never seen
Where staring malice never comes

I miss the heath its yellow furze
Molehills and rabbit tracks that lead   10
Through beesom ling and teazel burrs
That spread a wilderness indeed
The woodland oaks and all below
That their white powdered branches shield
The mossy pads*—the very crow   15
Croaked music in my native fields

I sit me in my corner chair
That seems to feel itself from home
I hear bird music here and there
From awthorn hedge and orchard come   20
I hear but all is strange and new
—I sat on my old bench in June
The sailing puddocks* shrill 'peelew'
Oer royce wood seemed a sweeter tune

I walk adown the narrow lane   25
The nightingale is singing now
But like to me she seems at loss
For royce wood and its shielding bough
I lean upon the window sill
The trees and summer happy seem   30
Green sunny green they shine—but still
My heart goes far away to dream

Of happiness and thoughts arise
With home bred pictures many a one
Green lanes that shut out burning skies   35
And old crooked stiles to rest upon

Above them hangs the maple tree
Below grass swells a velvet hill
And little footpads sweet to see
Goes seeking sweeter places still   40

With bye and bye a brook to cross
Oer which a little arch is thrown
No brook is here I feel the loss
From home and friends and all alone
—The stone pit with its shelving sides   45
Seemed hanging rocks in my esteem
I miss the prospect far and wide
From Langley bush and so I seem

Alone and in a stranger scene
Far from spots my heart esteems   50
The closen with their ancient green
Heath woods and pastures sunny streams
The hawthorns here were hung with may
But still they seem in deader green
The sun een seems to lose its way   55
Nor knows the quarter it is in

I dwell on trifles like a child
I feel as ill becomes a man
And still my thoughts like weedlings wild
Grow up to blossom where they can   60
They turn to places known so long
And feel that joy was dwelling there
So homebred pleasure fills the song
That has no present joys to heir

I read in books for happiness   65
But books mistake the way to joy
They change—as well give age the glass
To hunt its visage when a boy
For books they follow fashions new
And throw all old esteems away   70
In crowded streets flower never grew
But many there hath died away

Some sing the pomps of chivalry
As legends of the ancient time
Where gold and pearls and mystery   75
Are shadows painted for sublime
But passions of sublimity
Belong to plain and simpler things
And David underneath a tree
Sought when a shepherd Salems springs   80

Where moss did unto cushions spring
Forming a seat of velvet hue
A small unnoticed trifling thing
To all but heavens hailing dew
And Davids crown hath passed away   85
Yet poesy breaths his shepherd-skill
His palace lost and to this day
The little moss is blooming still

Strange scenes mere shadows are to me
Vague unpersonifying things   90
I love with my old hants* to be
By quiet woods and gravel springs

Where little pebbles wear as smooth
As hermits beads by gentle floods
Whose noises doth my spirits sooth   95
And warms them into singing moods

Here every tree is strange to me
All foreign things where ere I go
Theres none where boyhood made a swee
Or clambered up to rob a crow   100
No hollow tree or woodland bower
Well known when joy was beating high
Where beauty ran to shun a shower
And love took pains to keep her dry

And laid the shoaf* upon the ground   105
To keep her from the dripping grass
And ran for stowks* and set them round
Till scarce a drop of rain could pass
Through—where the maidens they reclined
And sun sweet ballads now forgot   110
Which brought sweet memorys to the mind
But here no memory knows them not

There have I sat by many a tree
And leaned oer many a rural stile
And conned my thoughts as joys to me   115
Nought heeding who might frown or smile
Twas natures beautys that inspired
My heart with rapture not its own
And shes a fame that never tires
How could I feel myself alone   120

No—pasture molehills used to lie
And talk to me of sunny days
And then the glad sheep resting bye
All still in ruminating praise
Of summer and the pleasant place   125
And every weed and blossom too
Was looking upward in my face
With friendship welcome 'how do ye do'

All tennants of an ancient place
And heirs of noble heritage   130
Coeval they with adams race
And blest with more substantial age
For when the world first saw the sun
These little flowers beheld him too
And when his love for earth begun   135
They were the first his smiles to woo

These little lambtoe bunches springs
In red tinged and begolden dye
For ever and like china kings
They come but never seem to die   140
These may-blooms with its little threads
Still comes upon the thorny bowers
And neer forgets those pinky heads
Like fairy pins amid the flowers

And still they bloom as in the day   145
They first crowned wilderness and rock
When abel haply crowned with may
The firstlings of his little flock

And Eve might from the matted thorn
To deck her lone and lovely brow   150
Reach that same rose that heedless scorn
Misnames as the dog rosey now

Give me no high flown fangled things
No haughty pomp in marching chime
Where muses play on golden strings   155
And splendour passes for sublime
Where citys stretch as far as fame
And fancys straining eye can go
And piled untill the sky for shame
Is stooping far away below   160

I love the verse that mild and bland
Breaths of green fields and open sky
I love the muse that in her hand
Bears wreaths of native poesy
Who walks nor skips the pasture brook   165
In scorn—but by the drinking horse
Leans oer its little brig to look
How far the sallows lean accross

And feels a rapture in her breast
Upon their root-fringed grains to mark   170
A hermit morehens sedgy nest
Just like a naiads summer bark
She counts the eggs she cannot reach
Admires the spot and loves it well
And yearns so natures lessons teach   175
Amid such neighbourhoods to dwell

I love the muse who sits her down
Upon the molehills little lap
Who feels no fear to stain her gown
And pauses by the hedgerow gap   180
Not with that affectation praise
Of song to sing and never see
A field flower grow in all her days
Or een a forests aged tree

Een here my simple feelings nurse   185
A love for every simple weed
And een this little shepherds purse
Grieves me to cut it up—Indeed
I feel at times a love and joy
For every weed and every thing   190
A feeling kindred from a boy
A feeling brought with every spring

And why—this 'shepherds purse' that grows
In this strange spot in days gone bye
Grew in the little garden rows   195
Of my old home now left—and I
Feel what I never felt before
This weed an ancient neighbour here
And though I own the spot no more
Its every trifle makes it dear   200

The ivy at the parlour end
The woodbine at the garden gate
Are all and each affections friend
That renders parting desolate

But times will change and friends must part   205
And nature still can make amends
Their memory lingers round the heart
Like life whose essence is its friends

Time looks on pomp with careless moods
Or killing apathys disdain   210
—So where old marble citys stood
Poor persecuted weeds remain
She feels a love for little things
That very few can feel beside
And still the grass eternal springs   215
Where castles stood and grandeur died

Decay

O POESY is on the wane
For fancys visions all unfitting
I hardly know her face again
Nature herself seems on the flitting
The fields grow old and common things   5
The grass the sky the winds a blowing
And spots where still a beauty clings
Are sighing 'going all a going'
O poesy is on the wane
I hardly know her face again   10

The bank with brambles over spread
And little molehills round about it
Was more to me then laurel shades
With paths and gravel finely clouted★

And streaking here and streaking there   15
Through shaven grass and many a border
With rutty lanes had no compare
And heaths were in a richer order
But poesy is in its wane
I hardly know her face again   20

I sat with love by pasture stream
Aye beautys self was sitting bye
Till fields did more then edens seem
Nor could I tell the reason why
I often drank when not a dry   25
To pledge her health in draught divine
Smiles made it nectar from the sky
Love turned een water into wine
O poesy is on the wane
I cannot find her face again   30

The sun those mornings used to find
When clouds were other-country-mountains
And heaven looked upon the mind
With groves and rocks and mottled fountains
These heavens are gone—the mountains grey   35
Turned mist—the sun a homeless ranger
Pursues a naked weary way
Unnoticed like a very stranger
O poesy is on its wane
Nor love nor joy is mine again   40

Loves sun went down without a frown
For every joy it used to grieve us
I often think that west is gone
Ah cruel time to undecieve us

The stream it is a naked stream   45
Where we on sundays used to ramble
The sky hangs oer a broken dream
The brambles dwindled to a bramble
O poesy is on its wane
I cannot find her haunts again   50

Mere withered stalks and fading trees
And pastures spread with hills and rushes
Are all my fading vision sees
Gone gone is raptures flooding gushes
When mushrooms they were fairy bowers   55
Their marble pillars overswelling
And danger paused to pluck the flowers
That in their swarthy rings were dwelling
But poesys spells are on the wane
Nor joy nor fear is mine again   60

Aye poesy hath passed away
And fancys visions undecieve us
The night hath taen the place of day
And why should passing shadows grieve us
I thought the flowers upon the hills   65
Were flowers from Adams open gardens
And I have had my summer thrills
And I have had my hearts rewardings
So poesy is on the wane
I hardly know her face again   70

And friendship it hath burned away
Just like a very ember cooling
A make believe on april day
That sent the simple heart a fooling

Mere jesting in an earnest way   75
Decieving on and still decieving
And hope is but a fancy play
And joy the art of true believing
For poesy is on the wane
O could I feel her faith again   80

Journey out of Essex[1]

JULY 18—1841—Sunday   Felt very melancholly—went a
walk on the forest in the afternoon—fell in with some gipseys
one of whom offered to assist in my escape from the mad
house by hideing me in his camp to which I almost agreed but
told him I had no money to start with but if he would do so
I would promise him fifty pounds and he agreed to do so
before saturday   on friday I went again but he did not seem
so willing so I said little about it—On Sunday I went and
they were all gone—an old wide awake hat and an old straw
bonnet of the plumb pudding sort was left behind—and I put
the hat in my pocket thinking it might be usefull for another
oppertunity as good luck would have it, it turned out to be so

July 19—Monday   Did nothing

July 20—Reconnitered the rout the Gipsey pointed out and
found it a legible one to make a movement and having only
honest courage and myself in my army I led the way and my
troops soon followed but being careless in mapping down the
rout as the Gipsey told me I missed the lane to Enfield town

[1] See Map, p. 208.

Northborough
:Glinton
·Werrington
Walton··
Peterborough
† Norman Cross
·Stilton

:Bugden
Ram Inn· St.Neot's

·Tamesford Turnpike
Gate
Potton·
··Biggleswade

Shefford
·Baldock
··Jack's
Hill
Stevenage

Enfield···
High
Beech
Ponders
End

Ten Miles Approximately

Clare's journey out of Essex, July 1841.

and was going down Enfield highway till I passed 'The
Labour in vain' Public house where a person I knew comeing
out of the door told me the way

I walked down the lane gently and was soon in Enfield
Town and bye and bye on the great York Road where it
was all plain sailing and stearing ahead meeting no enemy
and fearing none I reached Stevenage where being Night I got
over a gate crossed over the corner of a green paddock where
seeing a pond or hollow in the corner I forced to stay off a
respectable distance to keep from falling into it for my legs
were nearly knocked up and began to stagger   I scaled
some old rotten paleings into the yard and then had higher
pailings to clamber over to get into the shed or hovel which
I did with difficulty being rather weak   to my good luck I
found some trusses of clover piled up about 6 or more feet
square which I gladly mounted and slept on   there was some
trays in the hovel on which I could have reposed had I not
found a better bed   I slept soundly but had a very uneasy
dream   I thought my first wife lay on my left arm and
somebody took her away from my side which made me wake
up rather unhappy   I thought as I awoke somebody said
'Mary' but nobody was near—I lay down with my head
towards the north to show my self the steering point in the
morning

July 21—when I awoke daylight was looking in on every
side and fearing my garrison might be taken by storm and
myself be made prisoner I left my lodging by the way I got
in and thanked God for his kindness in procureing it (for any
thing in a famine is better than nothing and any place that
giveth the weary rest is a blessing)   I gained the north road
again and steered due north—on the left hand side the road
under the bank like a cave I saw a Man and boy coiled up

asleep which I hailed and they woke up to tell me the name
of the next village[1]

Some where on the London side the 'Plough' Public house
a Man passed me on horseback in a Slop frock and said 'here's
~~another of the broken down haymakers'~~ and threw me a
penny to get a half pint of beer which I picked up and
thanked him for and when I got to the plough I called for a
half pint and drank it and got a rest and escaped a very heavy
shower in the bargain by having a shelter till it was over—
afterwards I would have begged a penny of two drovers who
were very saucey so I begged no more of any body meet who
I would

I passed 3 or 4 good built houses on a hill and a public house
on the road side in the hollow below them   I seemed to pass
the Milestones very quick in the morning but towards night
they seemed to be stretched further asunder   I got to a
village further on and forgot the name   the road on the left
hand was quite over shaded by some trees and quite dry so I
sat down half an hour and made a good many wishes for
breakfast but wishes was no hearty meal so I got up as hungry
as I sat down—I forget here the names of the villages I passed
through but recollect at late evening going through Potton
in Bedfordshire where I called in a house to light my pipe in
which was a civil old woman and a young country wench
making lace on a cushion as round as a globe and a young
fellow all civil people—I asked them a few questions as to
the way and where the clergyman and overseer lived but they
scarcely heard me or gave me no answer[2]

[1] Baldeck [Clare's footnote; i.e. Baldock].
[2] Note. On searching my pockets after the above was written I found part
of a newspaper vide 'Morning Chronicle' on which the following fragments
were pencilled soon after I got the information from labourers going to work
or travellers journeying along to better their condition as I was hoping to do
mine in fact I believed I saw home in every ones countenance which seemed

I then went through Potton and happened with a kind talking country man who told me the Parson lived a good way from where I was or overseer I do'n't know which so I went on hopping with a crippled foot for a gravel had got into my old shoes one of which had now nearly lost the sole. Had I found the overseers house at hand or the Parsons I should have gave my name and begged for a shilling to carry me home but I was forced to brush on penny less and be thankfull I had a leg to move on—I then asked him wether he could tell me of a farm yard any where on the road where I could find a shed and some dry straw and he said yes and if you will go with me I will show you the place—its a public house on the left hand side the road at the sign of the 'Ram' but seeing a stone or flint heap I longed to rest as one of my feet was very painfull so I thanked him for his kindness and bid him go on— but the good natured fellow lingered awhile as if wishing to conduct me and then suddenly reccolecting that he had a hamper on his shoulder and a lock up bag in his hand cram full to meet the coach which he feared missing—he started hastily and was soon out of sight—I followed looking in vain for the countrymans straw bed—and not being able to meat it I lay down by a shed side under some Elm trees between the wall and the trees being a thick row planted some 5 or 6 feet from the buildings   I lay there and tried to sleep but the wind came in between them so cold that I lay till I quaked like the ague and quitted the lodging for a better at the Ram

---

so cheerful in my own—'There is no place like home' the following was written by the Roadside:—

    1st Day—Tuesday started from Enfield and slept at Stevenage on some clover trusses—cold lodging

    Wednesday—Jacks Hill is passed already consisting of a beer shop and some houses on the hill appearing newly built—the last Mile stone 35 Miles from London got through Baldeck and sat under a dry hedge and had a rest in lieu of breakfast.

which I could hardly hope to find—It now began to grow
dark apace and the odd houses on the road began to light up
and show the inside tennants lots very comfortable and my
outside lot very uncomfortable and wretched—still I hobbled
forward as well as I could and at last came to the Ram   the
shutters were not closed and the lighted window looked very
cheering but I had no money and did not like to go in   there
was a sort of shed or gighouse at the end but I did not like to
lie there as the people were up—so I still travelled on the road
was very lonely and dark in places being overshaded with trees

at length I came to a place where the road branched off into two turnpikes one to the right about and the other straight
forward and on going bye my eye glanced on a mile stone
standing under the hedge so I heedlessly turned back to read
it to see where the other road led too and on doing so I found
it led to London ˙ I then suddenly forgot which was North
or South and though I narrowly examined both ways I could
see no tree or bush or stone heap that I could reccolect I had
passed so I went on mile after mile almost convinced I was
going the same way I came and these thoughts were so strong
upon me that doubt and hopelessness made me turn so feeble
that I was scarcely able to walk yet I could not sit down or
give up but shuffled along till I saw a lamp shining as bright
as the moon which on nearing I found was suspended over a
Tollgate[1]   before I got through the man came out with a
candle and eyed me narrowly but having no fear I stopt to ask
him wether I was going northward and he said when you get
through the gate you are; so I thanked him kindly and went
through on the other side and gathered my old strength   as
my doubts vanished I soon cheered up and hummed the air
of Highland Mary as I went on   I at length fell in with an

[1] [There was a Turnpike Gate at Temsford or Tamesford or Tempsford,
four miles and six furlongs south of St. Neots.]

odd house all alone near a wood but I could not see what the
sign was though the sign seemed to stand oddly enough in a
sort of trough or spout   there was a large porch over the
door and being weary I crept in and glad enough I was to
find I could lye with my legs straight   the inmates were all
gone to roost for I could hear them turn over in bed as I lay
at full length on the stones in the porch—I slept here till
daylight and I felt very much refreshed as I got up—I blest
my two wives and both their familys when I lay down and
when I got up and when I thought of some former difficultys
on a like occasion I could not help blessing the Queen[1]   Having passed a Lodge on the left hand within a mile and half or
less of a town I think it might be[2] St. Ives but I forget the
name I sat down to rest on a flint heap where I might rest half
an hour or more and while sitting here I saw a tall Gipsey
come out of the Lodge gate and make down the road towards
where I was sitting   when she got up to me on seeing she
was a young woman with an honest looking countenance
rather handsome I spoke to her and asked her a few questions
which she answered readily and with evident good humour
so I got up and went on to the next town with her—she
cautioned me on the way to put somthing in my hat to keep

[1] MS 8, p. 25, contains the following note, written in a very disordered
hand which was due in all probability to a conjunction of fatigue and emotional
agitation:

The man whose daughter is the queen of England is now sitting on a stone
heap on the highway to bugden without a farthing in his pocket and without
eating a bit of food ever since yesterday morning—when he was offered a
bit of Bread and cheese at Enfield—he has not had any since but If I put a
little fresh speed on hope too may speed tomorrow—O Mary mary If you
knew how anxious I am to see you and dear Patty with the children I think
you would come and meet me

[This was presumably written late on Wednesday, 21st. Bugden was an
accepted variant of Buckden.]
[2] It was St. Neots [Clare's footnote].

the crown up and said in a lower tone 'you'll be noticed' but
not knowing what she hinted—I took no notice and made no
reply   at length she pointed to a small tower church which
she called Shefford Church and advised me to go on a foot-
way which would take me direct to it and I should shorten my
journey fifteen miles by doing so   I would gladly have
taken the young womans advice feeling that it was honest and
a nigh guess towards the truth but fearing I might loose my
way and not be able to find the north road again I thanked her
and told her I should keep to the road when she bade me
'good day' and went into a house or shop on the left hand
side the road   I have but a slight reccolection of my journey
between here and Stilton for I was knocked up and noticed
little or nothing—one night I lay in a dyke bottom from the
wind and went sleep half an hour when I suddenly awoke and
found one side wet through from the sock in the dyke bottom
so I got out and went on—I remember going down a very
dark road hung over with trees on both sides very thick which
seemed to extend a mile or two   I then entered a town and
some of the chamber windows had candle lights shineing in
them—I felt so weary here I forced to sit down on the ground
to rest myself and while I sat here a Coach that seemed to be
heavy laden came rattling up and stopt in the hollow below
me and I cannot reccolect its ever passing by me[1]   I then
got up and pushed onward seeing little to notice for the road
very often looked as stupid as myself and I was very often
half asleep as I went   on the third day I satisfied my hunger by
eating the grass by the road side which seemed to taste something like bread   I was hungry and eat heartily till I was
satisfied and in fact the meal seemed to do me good   the next

---

[1] Clare's marginal note: The Coach did pass me as I sat under some trees by
a high wall and the chips flew hard in my face and wakened me up from a doze
when I knocked the gravel out of my shoes and started.

and last day I reccolected that I had some tobacco and my box
of lucifers being exausted I could not light my pipe so I took
to chewing Tobacco all day and eat the quids when I had
done and I was never hungry afterwards—I remember
passing through Buckden and going a length of road afterwards but I dont reccolect the name of any place untill I came
to stilton where I was compleatly foot foundered and broken
down   when I had got about half way through the town a
gravel causeway invited me to rest myself so I lay down and
nearly went sleep a young woman (so I guessed by the voice)
came out of a house and said 'poor creature' and another more
elderly said 'O he shams' but when I got up the latter said 'o
no he dont' as I hobbled along very lame   I heard the voices
but never looked back to see where they came from—when
I got near the Inn at the end of the gravel walk I meet two
young women and I asked one of them wether the road
branching to the right by the end of the Inn[1] did not lead to
Peterborough and she said 'Yes' it did so as soon as ever I was
on it I felt myself in homes way and went on rather more
cheerfull though I forced to rest oftener then usual   before
I got to Peterborough a man and woman passed me in a cart
and on hailing me as they passed I found they were neighbours
from Helpstone where I used to live—I told them I was
knocked up which they could easily see and that I had neither
eat or drank anything since I left Essex   when I told my
story they clubbed together and threw me fivepence out
of the cart   I picked it up and called at a small public house
near the bridge were I had two half pints of ale and two-
penn'rth of bread and cheese   when I had done I started
quite refreshed only my feet was more crippled then ever and
I could scarcely make a walk of it over the stones and being
half ashamed to sit down in the street I forced to keep on the

[1] I.e. at Norman Cross, $5\frac{3}{4}$ miles to Peterborough.

move and got through Peterborough better then I expected when I got on the high road I rested on the stone heaps as I passed till I was able to go on afresh and bye and bye I passed Walton and soon reached Werrington and was making for the Beehive[1] as fast as I could when a cart met me with a man and woman and a boy in it when nearing me the woman jumped out and caught fast hold of my hands and wished me to get into the cart but I refused and thought her either drunk or mad but when I was told it was my second wife Patty I got in and was soon at Northborough   but Mary was not there neither could I get any information about her further then the old story of her being dead six years ago which might be taken from a bran new old Newspaper printed a dozen years ago but I took no notice of the blarney having seen her myself about a twelve month ago alive and well and as young as ever—so here I am homeless at home and half gratified to feel that I can be happy anywhere

> May none those marks of my sad fate efface
> For they appeal from tyranny to God
>
> Byron

July 24—1841—Returned home out of Essex and found no Mary—her and her family are nothing to me now though she herself was once the dearest of all—and how can I forget

from Child Harold

Now melancholly autumn comes anew
With showery clouds and fields of wheat tanned brown
Along the meadow banks I peace pursue
And see the wild flowers gleaming up and down

[1] Whellan's *Directory*, 1849, mentions only the *Cock*, the *Blue Bell*, the *Wheat Sheaf*, and the *Three Horse Shoes*.

Like sun and light—the ragworts golden crown   5
Mirrors like sunshine when sunbeams retire
And silver yarrow—there's the little town
And oer the meadows gleams that slender spire
Reminding me of one—and waking fond desire

I love thee nature in my inmost heart   10
Go where I will thy truth seems from above
Go where I will thy landscape forms a part
Of heaven—e'en these fens where wood nor grove
Are seen—their very nakedness I love
For one dwells nigh that secret hopes prefer   15
Above the race of women—like the dove
I mourn her abscence—fate that would deter
My hate for all things—strengthens love for her

Thus saith the great and high and lofty one
Whose name is holy—home eternity   20
In the high and holy place I dwell alone
And with them also that I wish to see
Of contrite humble spirits—from sin free
Who tremble at my word—and good receive
—Thou high and lofty one—O give to me   25
Truths low estate and I will glad believe
If such I am not—such I'm feign to live

That form from boyhood loved and still loved on
That voice—that look—that face of one delight
Loves register for years, months, weeks—time past and
   gone   30
Her looks was ne'er forgot or out of sight
—Mary the muse of every song I write

Thy cherished memory never leaves my own
Though cares chill winter doth my manhood blight
And freeze like Niobe my thoughts to stone—   35
Our lives are two—our end and aim is one

. . . .

Tis pleasant now days hours begin to pass
To dewy Eve—To walk down narrow close
And feel ones feet among refreshing grass
And hear the insects in their homes discourse   40
And startled blackbird flye from covert close
Of white thorn hedge with wild fears fluttering wings
And see the spire and hear the clock toll hoarse
And whisper names—and think oer many things
That love hurds up★ in truths imaginings   45

Fame blazed upon me like a comets glare
Fame waned and left me like a fallen star
Because I told the evil what they are
And truth and falshood never wished to mar
My Life hath been a wreck—and I've gone far   ·   50
For peace and truth—and hope—for home and rest
—Like Edens gates—fate throws a constant bar—
Thoughts may o'ertake the sunset in the west
—Man meets no home within a womans breast

Though they are blazoned in the poets song   55
As all the comforts which our lifes contain
I read and sought such joys my whole life long
And found the best of poets sung in vain   . ·
But still I read and sighed and sued again
And lost no purpose where I had the will   · 60
I almost worshiped when my toils grew vain
Finding no antidote my pains to kill
I sigh a poet and a lover still

Song

Dying gales of sweet even
How can you sigh so   65
Though the sweet day is leaving
And the sun sinketh low
How can you sigh so
For the wild flower is gay
And her dew gems all glow   70
For the abscence of day

Dying gales of sweet even
Breath music from toil
Dusky eve is loves heaven
And meets beautys smile   75
Love leans on the stile
Where the rustic brooks flow
Dying gales all the while
How can you sigh so

Dying gales round a prison   80
To fancy may sigh
But day here hath risen
Over prospects of joy
Here Mary would toy
When the sun it got low   85
Even gales whisper joy
And never sigh so

Labour lets man his brother
Retire to his rest
The babe meets its mother   90
And sleeps on her breast—
The sun in the west

Has gone down in the ocean
Dying gales gently sweep
O'er the hearts ruffled motion   95
And sing it to sleep

Song

No single hour can stand for nought
No moment hand can move
But calenders a aching thought
Of my first lonely love   100

Where silence doth the loudest call
My secrets to betray
As moonlight holds the night in thrall
As suns reveal the day

I hide it in the silent shades   105
Till silence finds a tongue
I make its grave where time invades
Till time becomes a song

I bid my foolish heart be still
But hopes will not be chid   110
My heart will beat—and burn—and chill
First love will not be hid

When summer ceases to be green
And winter bare and blea—
Death may forget what I have been   115
But I must cease to be

When words refuse before the crowd
My Marys name to give
The muse in silence sings aloud
And there my love will live   120

Now harvest smiles embrowning all the plain
The sun of heaven oer its ripeness shines
'Peace-plenty' has been sung nor sung in vain
As all bring forth the makers grand designs
—Like gold that brightens in some hidden mines   125
His nature is the wealth that brings increase
To all the world—his sun forever shines
—He hides his face and troubles they increase
He smiles—the sun looks out in wealth and peace

This life is made of lying and grimace   130
This world is filled with whoring and decieving
Hypocrisy ne'er masks an honest face
Story's are told—but seeing is believing
And I've seen much from which there's no retrieving
I've seen deception take the place of truth   135
I've seen knaves flourish—and the country grieving
Lies was the current gospel in my youth
And now a man—I'm further off from truth

I am

I AM—yet what I am, none cares or knows;
  My friends forsake me like a memory lost:
I am the self-consumer of my woes—
  They rise and vanish in oblivions host,
Like shadows in love frenzied stifled throes   5
  And yet I am, and live—like vapours tost

Into the nothingness of scorn and noise,
    Into the living sea of waking dreams,
Where there is neither sense of life or joys,
    But the vast shipwreck of my lifes esteems;   10
Even the dearest that I love the best
    Are strange—nay, rather, stranger than the rest.

I long for scenes where man hath never trod
    A place where woman never smiled or wept
There to abide with my Creator God,   15
    And sleep as I in childhood sweetly slept,
Untroubling and untroubled where I lie
    The grass below, above, the vaulted sky.

Sonnet
'I Am'

I FEEL I am, I only know I am
And plod upon the earth as dull and void
Earth's prison chilled my body with its dram
Of dullness, and my soaring thoughts destroyed.
I fled to solitudes from passions dream   5
But strife persued—I only know I am.
I was a being created in the race
Of men disdaining bounds of place and time—
A spirit that could travel o'er the space
Of earth and heaven—like a thought sublime,   10
Tracing creation, like my maker, free—
A soul unshackled like eternity,
Spurning earth's vain and soul debasing thrall
But now I only know I am—that's all.

Song

I WISH I was where I would be
With love alone to dwell
Was I but her or she but me
Then love would all be well
I wish to send my thoughts to her   5
As quick as thoughts can fly
But as the wind the waters stir
The mirrors change and flye

An invite to Eternity

WILT thou go with me sweet maid
Say maiden wilt thou go with me
Through the valley depths of shade
Of night and dark obscurity
Where the path hath lost its way   5
Where the sun forgets the day
Where there's nor life nor light to see
Sweet maiden wilt thou go with me

Where stones will turn to flooding streams
Where plains will rise like ocean waves   10
Where life will fade like visioned dreams
And mountains darken into caves
Say maiden wilt thou go with me
Through this sad non-identity
Where parents live and are forgot   15
And sisters live and know us not

Say maiden wilt thou go with me
In this strange death of life to be
To live in death and be the same
Without this life or home or name   20
At once to be and not to be
That was and is not—yet to see
Things pass like shadows—and the sky
Above, below, around us lie.

The land of shadows wilt thou trace   25
And look nor know each others face
The present mixed with reasons gone
And past and present all as one
Say maiden can thy life be led
To join the living with the dead   30
Then trace thy footsteps on with me
We're wed to one eternity

Sonnet

POETS love nature and themselves are love;
The scorn of fools and mock of idle pride
The vile in nature worthless deeds approve
They court the vile and spurn all good beside
Poets love nature like the calm of heaven   5
Her gifts like heaven's love spread far and wide
In all her works there are no signs of leaven
Sorrow abashes from her simple pride
Her flowers like pleasures have their seasons birth
And bloom through region here below   10

They are her very scriptures upon earth
And teach us simple mirth where e'er we go
Even in prison they can solace me
For where they bloom God is, and I am free.

A Vision

I LOST the love of heaven above
I spurned the lust of earth below
I felt the sweets of fancied love
And hell itself my only foe

I lost earth's joys but felt the glow   5
Of heaven's flame abound in me
Till loveliness and I did grow
The bard of immortality

I loved but woman fell away
I hid me from her faded fame   10
I snatched the sun's eternal ray
And wrote till earth was but a name

In every language upon earth
On every shore, o'er every sea,
I gave my name immortal birth,   15
And kept my spirit with the free
                          August 2nd 1844

Song

I HID my love when young while★ I
Coudn't bear the buzzing of a flye
I hid my love to my despite
Till I could not bear to look at light
I dare not gaze upon her face   5
But left her memory in each place
Where ere I saw a wild flower lye
I kissed and bade my love good bye

I met her in the greenest dells
Where dew drops pearl the wood blue bells   10
The lost breeze kissed her bright blue eye
The bee kissed and went singing bye
A sun beam found a passage there
A gold chain round her neck so fair
As secret as the wild bees song   15
She lay there all the summer long

I hid my love in field and town
Till e'en the breeze would knock me down
The Bees seemed singing ballads o'er
The flyes buss★ turned a Lions roar   20
And even silence found a tongue
To haunt me all the summer long
The riddle nature could not prove
Was nothing else but secret love

Clock a Clay★

IN THE cowslip's peeps I lye
Hidden from the buzzing fly
While green grass beneath me lies
Pearled wi' dew like fishes' eyes
Here I lie a Clock a clay   5
Waiting for the time o' day

While grassy forests quake surprise
And the wild wind sobs and sighs
My gold home rocks as like to fall
On its pillar green and tall   10
When the pattering rain drives bye
Clock a Clay keeps warm and dry

Day by day and night by night
All the week I hide from sight
In the cowslips peeps I lie   15
In rain and dew still warm and dry
Day and night and night and day
Red black spotted clock a clay

My home it shakes in wind and shows
Pale green pillar topt wi' flowers   20
Bending at the wild winds breath
Till I touch the grass beneath
Here still I live lone clock a clay
Watching for the time of day

[Martinmass]

Tis martinmass from rig to rig
Ploughed fields and meadow lands are blea
~~In hedge and field each restless twig~~
Is dancing on the naked tree
Flags in the dykes are bleached and brown   5
Docks by its sides are dry and dead
All but the ivy bows are brown
Upon each leaning dotterels head

Crimsoned with awes the awthorns bend
Oer meadow dykes and rising floods   10
The wild geese seek the reedy fen
And dark the storm comes oer the woods
The crowds of lapwings load the air
With buzes of a thousand wings
There flocks of sturnels too repair   15
When morning oer the valley springs

The crow sat on the willow

The Crow sat on the willow tree
A lifting up his wings
And glossy was his coat to see
And loud the ploughman sings
I love my love because I know   5
The milkmaid she loves me
And hoarsely croaked the glossy crow
Upon the willow tree
I love my love the ploughman sung
And all the field wi' music rung   10

I love my love a bonny lass
She keeps her pails so bright
And blythe she t[r]ips the dewy grass
At morning and at night
A cotton drab her morning gown   15
Her face was rosey health
She traced the pastures up and down
And nature was her wealth
He sung and turned each furrow down
His sweethearts love in cotton gown   20

My love is young and handsome
As any in the Town
She's worth a Ploughman's ransom
In the drab cotton gown
He sung and turned his furrows o'er   25
And urged his Team along
While on the willow as before
The old crow croaked his song
The ploughman sung his rustic Lay
And sung of Phebe all the day   30

The crow was in love no doubt
And wi a many things
The ploughman finished many a bout
And lustily he sings
My love she is a milking maid   35
Wi red and rosey cheek
O' cotton drab her gown was made
I loved her many a week
His milking maid the ploughman sung
Till all the fields around him rung   40

[How hot the sun rushes]

How hot the sun rushes
Like fire in the bushes
The wild flowers look sick at the foot of the tree
Birds nests are left lonely
The pewit sings only   5
And all seems disheartened, and lonely like me

Baked earth and burnt furrows
Where the rabbit he borrows
And yet it looks pleasant beneath the green tree
The crows nest look darkly   10
O'er fallows dried starkly
And the sheep all look restless as nature and me

Yet I love a meadow dwelling
Where nature is telling
A tale to the clear stream—its dearest to me   15
To sit in green shadows
While the herd turns to gadders
And runs from the hums of the fly and the bee

This spot is the fairest
The sweetest and rarest   20
This sweet sombre shade of the bright green tree
Where the morehens flag nest
On the waters calm breast
Lies near to this sweet spot thats been mother to me

Song

I'LL come to thee at even tide
When the west is streaked wi grey
I'll wish the night thy charms to hide
And daylight all away

I'll come to thee at set o' sun   5
Where white thorns i' the May
I'll come to thee when work is done
And love thee till the day

When Daisey stars are all turned green
And all is meadow grass   10
I'll wander down the bauk at e'en
And court the bonny Lass

The green banks and the rustleing sedge
I'll wander down at e'en
All slopeing to the waters edge   15
And in the water green

And theres the luscious meadow sweet
Beside the meadow drain
My lassie there I once did meet
Who I wish to meet again   20

The water lilies where in flower
The yellow and the white
I met her there at even's hour
And stood for half the night

23

SONG

We stood and loved in that green place   25
When sundays sun got low
Its beams reflected in her face
The fairest thing below

My sweet Ann Foot my bonny Ann
The Meadow banks are green   30
Meet me at even when you can
Be mine as you have been

NOTES

PAGE 56. PROSE ON CLARE'S READING. Clare's library is preserved at the Northampton Public Library and is listed in D. Powell, *Catalogue of the John Clare Collection in the Northampton Public Library*, Northampton, 1964. It contains some 440 volumes, many of which are editions of poetry such as Spenser's *Faery Queene*, Milton's *Paradise Lost*, Cowper, Gray etc. Clare was widely read in poetry, especially poetry of his own day and of the eighteenth century.

PAGE 67. THE PARISH. This long satirical poem has never been published in full, but we intend to rectify this in our O.E.T.S. edition. Some hundreds of lines, in a rather disjointed sequence, appear in J. Tibble (ed.), *Poems of John Clare*. Useful comparisons may be made with William Cobbett's *Autobiography*, but Clare's description is the most authentic and detailed portrait of village life and government surviving from the period.

PAGE 71.
113. *The Speaker: Or, Miscellaneous Pieces, Selected from the Best English Writers*, by William Enfield, Warrington, 1774, went into three more editions at least by 1790 and was a very popular anthology. Enfield, a Unitarian minister, had been a teacher at Warrington Academy and was a friend of Joseph Priestley.

PAGE 72.
151. *Squire Dandy just returnd from france* demonstrates the eighteenth-century tradition of the Grand Tour.

PAGE 73. PROSE ON THE OLD FARMER AND THE VICAR.

PAGE 75. A version of 'When this Old Hat was New' appears in G. Greig, *Folk Song of the North East*, Hatboro, Pennsylvania, 1963, Article 101; 'Toby Fillpot' can be found in M. W. Disher, *Victorian Song*, London, 1955, p. 68; 'Speed the Plough' is a well-known country dance. Clare's interest in songs and ballads is well described in M. Grainger, *John Clare: Collector of Ballads* (Peterborough Museum Society Occasional Papers, No. 3). Clare himself collected both words and tunes. The Librarian, Peterborough Museum Society, gives the following details:

'*Toby Fillpot* was written by Rev. F. Fawkes (1721–77) . . . He was a thirsty old soul who "among jolly topers bore off the bell". He died, whilst boozing in his arbour, "full as big as a Dorchester butt". His body turned to clay and from this a jug was made. (Hence "Toby Jug".)

> His body when long in the ground it had lain,
> And lime into clay had resolved it again,
> A potter found out in its covert so snug,
> And with part of fat Toby he formed this brown jug,
> Now sacred to friendship, to mirth and mild ale.
> So here's to my lovely sweet Nan of the Vale.'

(He suggests that this is the source of Clare's "Sweet patty of the Vale".)

PAGE 76. *healths out of glasses*: the whole of this passage showing the change of fashion in household goods is interesting for the student of the Industrial Revolution. Glasses replace 'drinking horns'; china, perhaps Wedgwood's, takes the place of brown earthenware; tea-drinking has become a regular social occasion for farmers' wives and daughters.

PAGE 77. *Moll Huggings*: possibly a mythical character, but see 'Valentine Eve' for Clare's interest in this kind of story.

PAGE 79. *Elliots Husbandry*: Jared Eliot, *Essays upon Field-Husbandry in New England, as it may be ordered*, Boston, 1760: given in *Bibliotheca Britannica* as Elliott, *Essays upon the Husbandry in New England*, London, 1764, 4to.
  '*George Barnwell*': *The London Merchant or the History of George Barnwell*, a play in prose by George Lillo (1693–1739) was first produced in 1731. It is a moralizing piece about the dangers of harlotry.

PAGE 79. *Old Tussers Husbandry*: Tusser, *Hundreth Good Pointes of Husbandry*, 1557, was amplified to *Five Hundreth Points of Good Husbandry United to as Many of Good Huswifery*, 1573.

PAGE 80. *great July flood; hot Wednesday:* the great July flood was probably the July of 1816. See *Gentleman's Magazine*, LXXXVI (2), 1816, pp. 76 and 173.
  'Hot Wednesday was 13 July 1808. The temperature rose to anything between 94° and 99°F in various parts of England. In Northamptonshire,

Constantia Orlebar said that it reached 92. Men were recorded to have
died in the fields as far north as Leicestershire.' (Professor G. Manley,
Department of Environmental Studies, University of Lancaster.)

PAGE 86. FIRST LOVES RECOLLECTIONS

PAGE 87.
   31. *Now nine years suns have risen and set*: this would appear to date
the poem in 1825 because Clare's last meeting with Mary seems to have
taken place in 1816. Clare saw Mary in the street in August 1821. (See
Clare's letter to John Taylor, 11 August 1821.)

PAGE 100. VALENTINE EVE. The story of this poem, suggested to
Clare, independently as it would seem, by both Edward Drury and
John Taylor, relates an actual historical occurrence. See *The Monthly
Magazine*, 1797, and E. Inglis-Jones, *The Lord of Burghley*, London,
1964.

PAGE 106.
197. *the postman*: at this date the postage on letters was paid by the
recipient and was expensive, often amounting to a shilling or more.
Clare was sometimes embarrassed by being obliged to pay postage on
letters in which he was not interested. The post then came to Market
Deeping, where Clare collected his letters, only once a week.

PAGE III.
   351. *And Oakley Hall that tops old Cromwells hill*: Clare is probably
thinking of Woodcroft Castle, occupied by the Bellairs family, old
friends of his. The castle had been held by the Royalists in the Civil
War. The king's chaplain, Dr. Michael Hudson, while trying to escape,
had his hands cut off as he hung from the battlements and was later
killed as he struggled out of the moat. The story is told by Sir Walter
Scott in *Woodstock*.

PAGE 113. *pilld*: the oak trees had been peeled of their bark which was
used in tanning in the local leather industries.
   Norman Cross Barracks, Huntingdonshire, housed French prisoners
from the Napoleonic Wars. See T. J. Wheeler, *The Depôt for Prisoners
of War at Norman Cross, Huntingdonshire, 1796–1816*, London, 1913.

PAGE 122. *Royce wood* is usually given on the maps as Rice Wood, but
it is claimed that Clare's spelling recalls the name of the farmer after
whom the wood was named.

PAGE 126. THE BADGER. The versions of this poem previously printed have omitted the first and second stanzas and differ in other particulars.

PAGE 129. THE MARTEN. This is the pine-marten.

PAGE 132. THE ROBIN. This stanza is taken from *The Shepherds Calendar*, 'December'. See David Lack, *The Life of the Robin* (Penguin). Clare anticipated many of the modern ornithologist's findings. Additional material on Clare as an ornithologist can be found in T. P. Harrison, *Birds in the Poetry of John Clare*, Peterborough Museum Society Occasional Papers, No. 1.

PAGE 134. A SUNDAY WITH SHEPHERDS AND HERDBOYS

PAGE 139.
    144. *A cromwell trench or roman mound*: the whole of the area between Stamford and Peterborough, and around Caistor is thick with material from the Roman period and from the Civil War. Clare shared anti-quarian interests with Artis and Henderson, two of Lord Fitzwilliam's house-servants.

PAGE 158. EMMONSAILS HEATH IN WINTER. This place was a familiar subject for Clare's poetry. See Tibble, *Poems*, i, 382–4.

PAGE 164. THE FLOOD.
    1. *Lolham Brigs*: half a dozen old stone arches carry the Roman road called King Street over the flood meadows of the Welland (Tibble, *Prose*, p. 110, note 2).

PAGE 173. A AUTUMN MORNING.
    1. '*One shower of cobwebs*': Clare may have been recalling the letter of 8 June 1775 in Gilbert White's *The Natural History of Selborne* (Every-man, pp. 164–6).

PAGE 186. SALTERS TREE. See Introduction, p. 15.

PAGE 190. APOLOGY FOR THE POOR. The dating of this passage from internal evidence is not so simple as it at first appears. Vansittart halved the leather duty in 1822 and Goulburn abolished the remainder in 1830. In 1825 there was a reduction in the spirits duty from 11s. 8¼d. to 7s. per gallon. Brougham attacked the excise on malt in 1822. In 1823 the intermediate Beer' Act was passed. A further Act of 1824 lowered licence rates for brewers at the lowest scale of production. In 1828 Estcourt's Comprehensive Licensing Bill was passed. There was a considerable debate about the malt and beer tax in 1826. See *Edinburgh Review*, September 1826. The passage may derive from 1829–30.

PAGE 204. DECAY. This poem is wrongly placed by Tibble among poems of the Helpstone period. It comes from the time when Clare had moved to Northborough.

PAGE 216. CHILD HAROLD. A complete text of this poem appears in our edition of *The Later Poems of John Clare*, Manchester, 1964. This book also contains our comments on Clare's asylum period. In 'Child Harold' the narrative stanzas have songs interspersed.

PAGE 221. I AM.
   6. '*tost*': this is an emendation. The Knight Transcripts read 'lost'.

GLOSSARY

a	On, as in 'a foot'; in, or at, as in 'a church'.
awe	Var. of *haw*.
ball	Ball, traditional name for an ox.
bandy	The knobbed stick used to strike the ball in games such as hockey. See *clink*.
bate	To teaze or worry. N.i.B. (i.e. not recorded by Baker).
bauk	Var. of *baulk*.
baulk	The unploughed strip between ploughed fields or furrows.
beavering hour	Time for refreshment, used especially of harvesting and haymaking.
bent	Coarse grass.
blea	Exposed and cold.
bottle of flags	A bundle of osiers or reeds. 'Bottle is also applied to a bundle of sticks collected from the hedges for firing.' The term is still used by thatchers.
brake	Fern.
breath	Var. of *breathe*.
brig	Var. of *bridge*.
brunt	Wright gives 'to turn' or 'to stop', but in Clare the context suggests an abrupt or forceful movement. N.i.B.
brustle	To bustle about, make a great fuss or stir. N.i.B.
budget	A bag, pack, or wallet, generally of leather;

especially a tinker's wallet and the pouch in which a mower carries his whetstone.

bumbarrel The long-tailed tit.

burr 1. *Verb.* To slow a wheel down by friction.

2. *Sub.* A halo round the moon, usually betokening rain.

buss 1. A kiss.

2. A variant of *buzz*.

cag A small cask or keg. N.i.B.

checkering Creating a pattern like that of a chequer or chessboard.

chelping chirping.

chickering 'An imitative word expressive of the cricket's cry'. *Baker.*

chock The game of marbles played by chocking or pitching marbles into a hole instead of shooting at a ring.

cirging Surging. More likely to be the word in the manuscript than the weaker 'urging'.

clammed Parched with thirst, or sometimes starved with hunger.

claum In Wright, this occurs only as a verb, to seize or clutch with decided grasp. N.i.B.

clink As in *clink and bandy chock*; 'clink' may be onomatopoeic, expressive of the contact of marble; alternatively, it may signify 'clench' in which case 'clink and bandy chock' may denote marbles played by first 'clenching' the thumb and then allowing it, on release, to strike the marble as the bandy or hockey stick strikes the ball.

clock To clip-clop: onomatopoeic; N.i.B.

clock-a-clay	The lady-bird or lady-cow.
closen	The plural form of *close*.
clouted	Clothed or patched.
clown	A rustic.
cotter	Var. of *cottager*.
courtseys	Curtseys. Shows the origin of the word from 'courteseys'.
covert	cover't = cover'it.
coyed	Decoyed.
crab	Crab apple.
crack	To boast or jest.
crane	As in 'act the crane': 'A man holds in his hand a long stick, with another tied at the top in the form of an L reversed, which represents the long neck and beak of the crane. This, with himself, is entirely covered with a large sheet. He mostly makes excellent sport, as he puts the whole company to the rout, picking out the young girls, and pecking at the bald heads of the old men . . .'. Clare's description in the Introduction to *The Village Minstrel*, 1821.
crank	Twisted, crooked. N.i.B.
crimpled	Wrinkled, crumpled.
crimping	A succession of small folds, frills or flutings.
crizzle	To crisp or crystallize; used of water that is beginning to freeze.
crizzling	Onomatopoeic use of the word, suggestive of gnawing.
cronk	To croak or honk, used especially of frogs and geese.
croodling	Contracting the body from cold, shrinking or huddling.

cross plumb skittles Probably the game where there is
(*a*) a cross, or support (stake or post); (*b*) a
plumb-weight on a string attached to the
cross-piece and allowed to swing and hit
the skittles. N.i.B.

cross-row Christ-cross-row = alphabet. Therefore 'as
plain as the alphabet'.

crumping Making a crunching sound, as frozen snow
when it yields to the feet.

dab To strike.

dimute Var. of *diminute*, diminished.

doll Doll: traditional name for a milkmaid.

dotterel A pollard-tree; 'old stumping trees in hedge
rows, that are headed or lopped every ten
or twelve years for fire-wood'. Clare.

douse to soak or drench.

drabbled Draggled, smeared, muddied.

drowking Drooping from drought.

ducking stone 'Ducks' is a boys' game, played with three
stones, surmounted by a fourth, which the
player tries to dislodge by throwing at it
from a short distance.

eke To add to, to increase.

eldern Pl. of elder.

flaze flaring, as a candle when a current of air
causes it to burn unsteadily.

flirt To flit or flutter.

flusker To fly with sudden motion, with an element
of noise and commotion.

fodder To feed.

fother To feed.

fotherer   One who brings fodder.

foulroyce   Foul-rush, the dogwood or spindle-tree, i.e. either *Cornus sanguinea* or *Euonymus europaens*.

frail   Flail.

fret   To thaw.

frumitory   Frumenty, a dish made of hulled wheat boiled in milk and seasoned.

furze kidder   a person who collects and makes up bundles of furze, or furze-kids.

gadders   Restless movement, as of cows pestered by the gad-fly.

gadding   Moving in a restless, excited fashion.

gale   Breeze.

gangs   Goes.

glabber   To jabber, chatter. Clare's use may well be metaphorical.

goss   common furze, gorse.

gough   To gouge; cf. Clare's use of hugh for huge: also *sb*. gouge.

grain   A larger branch of a tree.

green-sickness An anaemic disease mostly affecting young women about the age of puberty and giving a pale or greenish tinge to the complexion: *chlorosis*.

grubbed   Uprooted; the grub-axe was part axe and part hoe.

hants   Var. of *haunts*.

hariff   Var. of *hairif*, *hayrif*; cleavers or goose-grass, *Galium aparine*.

heir long   Heirloom.

hing	To hang.
hirkle	To crouch, to set up the back, as cattle who shrink from cold.
hirple	To limp.
hollow	Var. of *holler*, *holla*.
hugh	Clare's spelling of *huge*.
hurd up	To hoard.
huzzing	clamorous, tumultuous.
icle	Icicle.
idless	Var. of *idleness*.
ingenious	Ingenuous, here ignorant.
Joe Millar	An old joke. Cf. *Joe Miller's Jest Book*, 5th edn., 1742.
joll	To walk lumberingly along.
knarl	To gnaw, nibble.
knewt	Newt.
land	An arable division of a furlong in an open field.
lare	To rest in a shelter.
ling	Heath; *Calluna vulgaris*.
loose	Clare's spelling of *lose*.
lown	Var. of *loon*.
lunge	To lurch, to hide, to skulk.
on the lurch	Lurking, in order to surprise.
mere mark	Meer: a strip or slip of grass land, serving as a boundary to different properties, or as a division of parishes in open fields.
mizled	Wet with mizzle or drizzle.
morts	Great numbers.
mouldiwarp	The mole.

muscle   Clare's spelling of *mussel*.
nail passer   Corruption of nail-piecer: i.e. auger or gimlet.
near   Clare's spelling of *ne'er*.
nimble   To move nimbly.

---

oddling   One differing from the rest of a family, brood, or litter; generally applied to the smallest, or to one with a peculiarity.

pad   Var. of *path*.
pelt   To throw at.
pendil   Pendle-stone: a name given by quarry-men to the upper course in a stone-pit; in the quarries of Kingsthorpe, the hard blue stone was called the pendle-stone; used as a whetstone, especially for sharpening sickles and scythes.
pess   To soak; cf. piss.
pill   To peel or strip off.
pinder   A person employed to impound stray cattle.
pink   The chaffinch.
pismire   The ant.
platt   A flat stretch of ground.
pluft   Swollen, bloated, puffy; an epenthesis of *puffed*.
poesy   Clare's spelling of *posey*.
pooty   The girdled snail-shell; *Helix nemoralis*.
popples   Poplars.
prank   To adorn or decorate.
pranking   Frolicsome. N.i.B.
prevade   Var. of *pervade*.
prog   To poke or prod.
protentious   Portentous.

puddock	The name applied indiscriminately in Northants to the fan-tail kite or buzzard and to the forked-tail kite.
pudgy	Full of puddles; Baker gives *pudge* as a diminutive of *puddle*.

quaking or quawking   Cawing.

ramp	To romp; to rampage; to grow luxuriantly.
rawky	Misty, foggy.
reak	To emit steam or vapour.
reciept	Recipe.
reek	Var. of *reak*.
ride	A riding: open space or road in a wood.
rig	Ridge.
rock	To sway, to walk unsteadily.
rotten	Rotten wood.
rout	Clare uses the same word for 'route' or 'rout' and therefore it seems to share a little of both senses wherever it occurs.

sallow	Species of *Salix*.
sawn	To saunter.
sawney	Idle.
scratt	Var. of *scratch*.
scrip	A shepherd's coat, generally made of leather.
scrowed	Marked or scratched, in lines.
shill	Shrill.
shoaf	Sheaf.
shool	To saunter lazily.
shoves	Sheaves.
shoy	Shy.

sicken	Mope.
sinkfoil	Cinquefoil, probably *Potentilla reptans*.
slive	To slide or slip past.
slove	Pret. of *slive*.
sluther	To slide, slither.
small swipes	small beer.
snob	A shoemaker or cobbler.
snuft	To snuffle or sniff.
soodle	To saunter.
spirey	Pointed and tapering, like a spire.
sprent	Sprinkled.
sprotes	Small twigs, for firewood.
sputter	To run up quickly, with a commotion.
startle	To start, as in surprise, to be in a great bustle.
stick	To decorate.
stingo	Stronge ale or beer.
stiver	A coin of small value.
stools	The exposed roots of trees.
stouk	Stook.
stowk	Stook.
streak	To stretch.
on the strunt	Strutting.
struttle	Minnow or stickleback.
stulp	Stump.
sturnel	Starling.
sturt	To start, to shake suddenly.
sutty	Clare's spelling of sooty.
swail	swale, shade.
swath	A range or row of cut grass or corn, as it falls from the scythe.
swea	See *swee*.
swee	Swaying, rocking. Cf. see-saw.
swift	This word occurs later in the selection and

refers to the same creature, the common newt or eft.

swop   To swoop or pounce.

taws   Marbles.
teem   To empty, to pour out.
then   Clare's consistent form of *than*.
throstle   The song-thrust or missel-thrush.
trace   To walk.
tray   Hurdle.
tutle   Clare's spelling of *tootle*.
twank   A shorter, sharper, variant of *twang*.

watchet   sky blue.
wear   To persevere in.
were   Clare's almost consistent spelling of *where*.
wetting   Whetting.
whew   The cry of the owl.
while   Until.
whimpling   Wimpling, rippling, meandering.
wift   Whift, or whiff; a puff of smoke as from a pipe.
wimble   A gimlet or auger.
without side On the outside.

yaum   Var. of yealm, a prepared layer of wetted straw for thatching, about eighteen inches by five inches.
yaumd   (Of beans): cut carefully and gathered into a manageable sheaf of about the same size and shape as a thatcher's yealm.
younker   Youngster.